HOW THIS BOOK WORKS

Buying and selling are two sides of the same coin: to understand one, you need to understand the other. This flip book works the same way. Read this side to learn about selling, then flip the book upside down to see the world from the opposite perspective of buying. Good news: they meet in the middle.

WHO IS THIS BOOK FOR

The ideas in this book really only apply to people buying and selling fairly expensive stuff. That means you're solving problems in mid-to-large size companies with typical deal values of at least $50,000. The insights apply to any industry, not just venture-funded software companies. That said, a lot of the innovation around buyer-seller collaboration comes from SaaS, so apologies in advance if any tech jargon slipped through.

ABOUT TOM

After 23 years of sales & marketing inside startups, enterprise software, electronics manufacturing and marketing agencies, Tom is focused on making the global economy slightly more efficient by improving how we buy and sell.

Tom was co-founder of DealPoint, the first sales collaboration solution for customer-centric sales teams. He sold to Clari, the folks who created the revenue operations category and who now make the best revenue platform in the industry.

Tom talks, listens, parents and squashes in Portland, Oregon and Brighton, England.

SLIGHTLY MORE EFFICIENT

SELLING

A practical guide to finding the people with the problems you fix,
then helping them evaluate why they should buy from you

Tom Williams

Common Foreword

Buying and selling are two sides of the same coin, so why are there so few books about buying? And how could you even write about one without referencing the other?

I don't know, so this book has two front covers. Read this side to learn about selling, then flip the book upside down to see the world from the opposite perspective of buying. Good news: they meet in the middle.

At the end of the day, if someone learns they have a problem, then they have exactly three options: they can do nothing, they can fix it themselves, or they can find a partner to help them.

Buyers are people who find themselves needing to make this decision. Sellers are people whose job is to help buyers evaluate those options, admittedly with a strong bias towards option C.

My goal with this book is to make that process slightly more efficient. I believe we'll do this by being more open with each other about how best to work together. I also believe if we get it right, then we can literally boost the global economy and bump human productivity by a couple points. No pressure!

You can read this book as either a buyer or a seller, but ideally, you'll read both sides to understand how your counterparty thinks. My only ask is that you use this knowledge for good. Don't go ripping off the other side just because I told you what they're thinking.

Tom Williams, Portland, August 2024

CONTENTS — SELLING SIDE

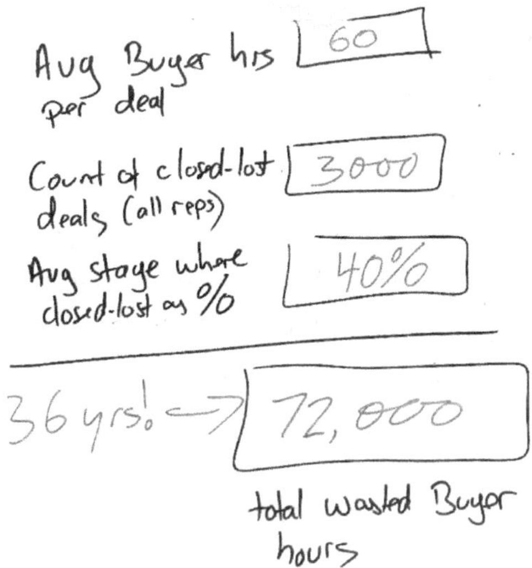

INTRODUCTION | Slightly More Efficient

Figuring out if you can help a customer is the fastest path to quota

If a typical win rate for an enterprise sales team is 20%, that means the other 80% of deals were wasted time. As sellers, we may be willing to pay that price to find the gold in the dirt, but for every one of the deals in that 80%, there was at least one buyer whose time was wasted too.

If we collaborate better, sellers AND buyers will waste less time and the global economy will be slightly more efficient.

What you do with your share of that efficiency is up to you: more deals, more time with your family, or maybe a bit of both.

Becoming slightly more efficient

Becoming Slightly More Efficient is all about minimizing the time and effort it takes to figure out three things. If you can't deliver on all three then there's no deal.

1   **Does the customer have a problem that is urgent and important?**
There is a problem in their business, either in their role or in how they compete in their industry. They're aware of the problem. It's worth fixing. It shouldn't wait.

2   **Can you solve the problem faster or more reliably than they could do it themselves?**
You need to know something or have something that the buyer doesn't have or doesn't know. Otherwise, why wouldn't they just do it themselves?

3   **Can you convince the customer that the first two things are true?**
Your business case wraps the first two things into a single package that your buyers will either believe or disbelieve.

In addition to saving time on the deal at hand, if we follow these ideas we'll kill a lot of the bad selling where sellers use charm and deceit to sell something the buyer doesn't really need. That kind of selling leads to even more wasted time where the customer is trying to make their investment work, then even more even more time unwinding the damage done.

We can all do better.

A couple definitions

I'll be referring back to **urgent and important problems** over and over across both sides of this book, so before we get into it, let's take a minute and really think about the concept.

A leaky pipe that leaks $1000 of water per month is an important problem to fix. But it's less urgent than a pipe at risk of suddenly bursting and gushing $10,000 a day. Sure you should fix that first pipe, but it can wait til the second one is fixed. A third pipe doesn't leak at all, but it's narrow so it takes ages to get water from A to B. It's a source of daily irritation for the workers and it's inefficient, but doesn't actually cost anything.

A new pipe would fix each of these problems. But only one is urgent *and* important. And that's the only one that's likely to get replaced anytime soon.

I'm also going to talk about a Point of View a lot. Understanding something about the buyer's business is the only way to know if they have a problem that you can help fix. What does dripping water do to factory equipment? How do slippery floors affect employee safety? What common additives in factory coolant systems are known to corrode pipes?

Knowledge about the thing you sell won't cut it. With a point of view (or POV) about their situation, you can talk confidently about the root causes of their problem, get into the costs of acting or ignoring, and have an enlightened, two-way conversation about the different ways they might think about finding a fix. You show up more as a credible consultant, and you'll find it much easier to diagnose their problem and recommend a solution that actually solves.

In short: if you have a thoughtful POV that helps you find and fix urgent & important problems, you're 95% of the way to making your corner of the world slightly more efficient.

CHAPTER 1 | Buyers' Book of Tricks

What the other side will try

Over on the buyer side of this book, I share all the tricks I've seen sellers do to try to push buyers to buy.

I did this because if buyers know the tricks, I'm hoping sellers will be forced to cut out the techniques and focus instead on the fundamentals of being a partner to the customer, finding a problem and figuring out if you can help them fix it.

But buyers are no saints. They have their own selection of tricks to get a leg up. Hopefully by knowing each other's chicanery, you'll both cut out the power plays and just work together.

Most of the buyer's tricks come later in the sales process during negotiation, but there are still things they'll do in discovery.

Try to remember that most of this shadiness stems from the buyer's lack of trust in you, the seller. The faster you show you're trustworthy and actually offering real value, the sooner they'll stop wasting all this time and effort trying to protect themselves from you and what you might do to them.

Discovery & other pre-negotiation tricks

1. **The Stooge**
2. **Fibbing on budget**
3. **Pilot instead of professional services**

1. The Stooge

This is a trick that starts at the very first engagement and is the quintessential waste of your time. The buyer already has a vendor in mind, but either they've been ordered to find a second quote, or they want some leverage to pressure a vendor they're already working with. So they reach out to you and ask for a price quote. Look for a "champion" who's unwilling to intro you to others on the buyer committee, unwilling to invest time in discovery or a mutual action plan, and who keeps coming back to just getting a price out of you.

The thing is, a confident customer can have the same profile. They don't want to do discovery because they already understand their problem and they know how they want to fix it.

If you're suspicious that they're wasting your time, ask if they're working with a preferred vendor already and gauge their reaction. If you've established any kind of personal relationship, you can just ask them person-to-person what the situation is.

If they're serious buyers insisting on price early on, then promise to give a ballpark range, but explain you need to know a little more to give an accurate price. If you have any personal rapport, remind them that having an expert's perspective on their problem can only help (that expert being not just you, but your entire team). Your team has seen it all, and you might know something they don't. Only way to tell is walking through the problem. A serious buyer looking to fix a problem should be willing to share.

If they're not serious, just give a much broader price range and tell them you can't do anything more to help them until they share some more information. You can either look for a more open champion or be strong, mark it closed-lost and move on.

2. Fibbing on budget

Every buyer will plead poverty if you ask what their budget is. They know that you're going to ask for 100% of what they have, so they low-ball you. It's so expected, it's almost not shady. What's more, if you're coming to them cold, then the answer is zero budget has been allocated.

This trick is actually a consequence of you posing the wrong question. Asking about budget to buy your product is inviting a fib. Why would I have budget to buy something I don't need?

It's more helpful to ask if they've budgeted to fix this problem, or how they usually fund similarly-sized initiatives this person has been involved with. That'll give you a much more insightful view of how seriously they're taking this problem, where they are in the process and where your budget request stands against the other priorities they could spend their money on.

3. Pilot instead of Professional Services

A pilot program is where a buyer asks to test your service to make sure it'll all go as promised.

That's a totally reasonable request if the other forms of proof of value (references, deep demos etc.) won't work. The trick they can play is when you have to do some setup or configuration to get the product or service working.

When someone buys, it's pretty common to charge for any implementation work as a paid-for Professional Services engagement. The problem with pilots is that even if it's paid, it's really hard to charge the full cost of a proper implementation. So you waive the PS charges just to get the pilot up and running.

The trick comes when they buy: they say 'no thanks' to the professional services component of your quote because they already got most of it set up during the pilot.

More than the money, this goes to the inherent risk of pilots.

If either one of you only half-commits to the pilot (in your case running with a "light" implementation; in their case not really using the software during the pilot), you're going to get less-than-stellar results, and now you're in a substantially worse negotiating position because they didn't see the results you'd promised. This is 100% your fault.

Avoid falling into this trap by designing a pilot that doesn't require professional services to demonstrate success.

More on this later.

Negotiation & procurement tricks

1. **Procurement renegotiation**
2. **Initial order with promised volume later**
3. **Early Escape Clause**
4. **Scope Creep**
5. **Most Favored Customer**
6. **Cost Plus**
7. **Net 90 terms**
8. **Writing the contract on their paper**
9. **Expecting expired discounts to be honored**

1. Procurement renegotiation

This is the worst. You negotiate with your champion to arrive at a price that works for both of you, then just as you think you're all done, Procurement enters the fray reopening the negotiation with a demand for further discount.

There are three counter moves here.

First, figure out who's who. If your deal is worth more than $20K, there will be multiple people involved. During discovery, ask if your champion or executive sponsor has final signature authority, find out who else will need to sign off on what you agree. Then make a point to ask what the role of Procurement will be.

Get that discussion in writing and include it in your Mutual Action Plan. Continue to validate and re-validate throughout the process. It has been known for champions to fib and say they have approval authority when actually they're just a recommender.

Second, from the very first moment of price discussion, be open about your price levers.

The idea here is rather than just giving up percentages of the proposal, show how your discounting works. Use the concept of "give and get". You'll *give* a discount if you *get* something like more volume, longer term, or earlier start date.

Document the give-and-get you did with your champion or the executive sponsor, so when Procurement comes in hot asking for discount, you can show how you already applied X and Y discounts, and that the only remaining lever is Z, which you're happy to give in return for a get.

By no means will this work every time, so number three here is the biggie.

Third and most important — trust in your value and use your advocates inside the buyer organization to defend your pricing for you.

At the end of the day, pricing really comes down to the cost of their problem divided by how much they believe you. Massive value fixing an urgent problem and 100% credibility? Procurement won't dare get in the way. Call your buyer executive sponsor, and tell them that Procurement is blocking the urgent and important problem from being fixed.

Don't have an exec sponsor? You're in trouble. Don't make the same mistake next time.

2. Initial order with promised volume later

The buyer says "I want 10,000 units." You offer a great price, then they say "actually I want that price, but let's start with 1000 units".

Hold the line by explaining the volume lever again or offer a compromise by contracting the 10,000 delivered over time, paid as the units are delivered.

3. Early Escape Clause

Some companies will ask for a discount in return for accepting a multi-year term, but then add an early termination cause with zero penalty. This takes all the risk off the customer and puts it all on you. It's actually riskier than a normal one year term because your renewal systems won't catch that they could quit early, and you might end up surprised after thinking that you had more time to prove value.

You can either reject this request out of hand and just go for a single year at single year pricing, or insist on a metric to measure that first year's performance. If you miss, they can get out. But again, that puts all the risk on you. You're supposed to be partners, so put this on the table: Agree a metric of success with three levels from "unhappy" to "meets expectation" to "exceeds expectation". If you miss, they can terminate or even get some percent refunded; if you exceed expectation, then they pay you a bonus. Confidence on a stick!

4. Scope Creep

This happens when the buyer agrees to a certain feature requirement or implementation criteria, then never accepts the work as complete with an endless list of last minute additions. This is much more likely to happen to companies who don't provide clear expectations on what they're delivering.

Counter this trick by (a) being really specific on what you're going to deliver and (b) specifying a set number of revisions and a per-hour or per-turn charge for anything after the agreed number of revisions. As a seller, you have to be self-aware enough to recognize when it's your side's fault. If the buyer's complaints are valid, then every additional turn makes the situation worse as they lose more and more faith and inspect everything more and more closely.

5. Most Favored Customer

I've seen this most often with the US Federal Government, but other large organizations will do it too. They insert a clause in your agreement where you promise that you've never sold this product to anyone else for a cheaper price, and that if you ever do in the future, you'll reduce their price accordingly.

If you're transparent with your pricing levers, this should be a total dud, since you can show how your pricing is defined. If you want to fight fire with fire, then create a unique SKU and make what you're selling substantively unique so you can say with (legal) assurance "no one else gets this SKU for any cheaper than you."

Being transparent about your pricing and value is the better approach though.

6. Cost Plus

I had a customer demand that we share our COGS (cost of goods sold) info and then they'd give us 5% over that cost. We told them to take a hike. We were only able to do this because we knew the time & budget it would take for them to create their own solution or bring a different vendor up to our quality level. Without killer discovery and confidence that it would cost them a bomb to try and fix their problem in-house, we might not have been able to call their bluff.

7. Net 90 terms

You've negotiated in good faith, you've got to the final figure, and they throw some crazy Net 90 terms on you. Big companies do this all the time, making smaller companies provide free bridge loans at zero percent interest. I've even seen companies put Net 60 on their invoice, then take 2% off the bill for paying on time. They know you're not going to complain.

The antidote to all these terms tricks is to get a pro forma contract in front of the customer early in the negotiation so you have time to read any edits they're trying to sneak in and push back. Don't bother trying to get procurement to back down. Get your champion to pull in the executive sponsor and apply pressure from the top inside the buying org.

8. Writing the contract on their paper

It might not seem like a big deal, but if you agree to the contract on their paper (ie using their contract terms or their MSA), you're going to end up on the back foot. Look for perpetual license or IP ownership clauses that could cause you a headache months or years from now. Even best case, now your team has to manage two sets of documents for the rest of your time working together.

As a rep, your only recourse here is to lean on your legal team and push for using your standard contract, but this can be hard if you're in a David < Goliath situation.

9. Expecting expired discounts to be honored

I understand this one. You offer a discount to get them to move on your timeline instead of theirs (ie: end of quarter). They don't pull the trigger, then on the second day of the new quarter, they ask for the same price. The problem here is they know you're willing to do that price. More important, they know you believe your value is that much less than you originally stated.

The counter here is to bring in your own bad cop. When you're making the offer, include your ice-cold Deal Desk folks so everyone is clear this is a one-time-offer, and then lean on Deal Desk to be the enforcer. Better yet, don't offer desperate deals at the end of the quarter.

At the end of the day, all these tricks are a distraction from the real question: does the customer have an urgent and important problem, and can you help fix it for less money or with less risk than them ignoring the problem or fixing it themselves.

If they're not willing to work with you to answer those two questions, then first try giving them the benefit of doubt and assume it's because they don't trust you yet. That's something you can change.

If it's a negotiation issue, then call it out and offer to go review the value they think they'll be getting and the risk they think they'd be taking on.

If they really are just playing games, then you have to decide if it's worth your time to keep playing. Maybe you just give them the quote, the discount, the free PS and do better next time.

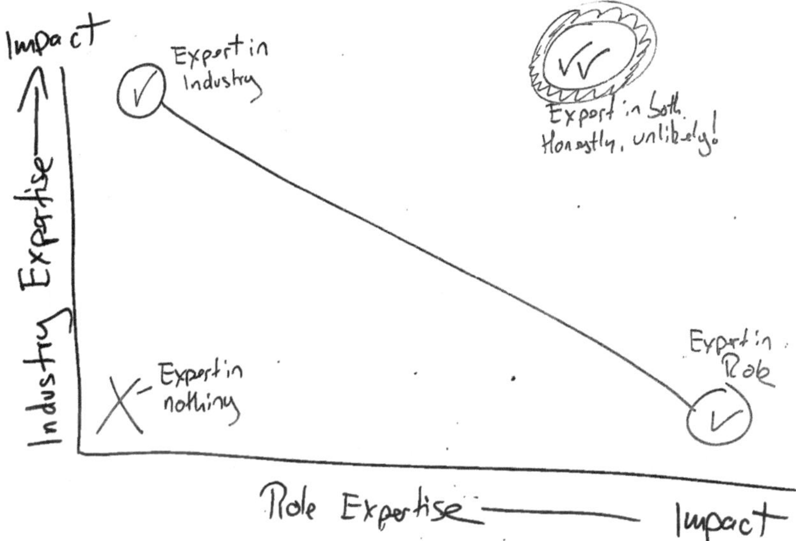

CHAPTER 2 | Own your POV

What do you know that no one else knows?

A point of view, or POV, is your secret knowledge. It's how you see the world differently than your customers and competitors. It might be something about a specific industry, or it might be something about a specific business process, but knowing what you know gives you an edge.

A POV is not your product. It's the understanding of why one approach works better than another. It's the ability to recognize patterns in novel situations, and the ability to explain those patterns in your own words.

It's your personal framework to deal with the world: it's what you know and believe.

Armed with a strong POV, you'll stand tall above competitors, your buyers will listen and you'll be able to figure out really fast whether they have the kind of problem you can solve.

Your POV has to be relevant to your customer, and specifically, it has to be relevant to an important and urgent problem your customer is experiencing.

The final requirement is that you can show a clear path connecting the dots from the buyer's problem to your POV to solving their problem. If that path is too complicated or too convoluted, or even just too academic to explain to your buyer, then it's not a good POV.

Challenger calls these your commercial insights, but I think there's more to it than a set of words that you memorized. To be useful and transferable, those insights have to be wrapped in a narrative, a model of the world that will let you recognize and deconstruct a buyer's problem even if you've never seen that exact version of it before.

If you're an individual contributor and you don't have a formal POV coming down from leadership, you need to make one up. This is less about creating a completely new way of thinking about the world and more about assimilating what's already in your company's collateral and really making it your own.

Crafting a POV isn't easy, but it's worth the effort. Having a POV makes you stand out from the crowd to prospects, confers authority and confidence to stand up to the customer's senior decision makers and gives you a framework to reframe their problem on your terms.

Having a POV takes the discussion out of feature comparison land and into business strategy, where no competitor can touch you. Ultimately it will help you figure out if you can actually help the customer, so you can disqualify bad prospects out of your pipe earlier, spend more time on the good deals, and at the end negotiate from a position of power.

Right now it might feel like a ton of work, but you should be able to get to 80% confidence in just a few hours over a week or two.

1. Take inventory

Spend 4-8 hours reading everything you can that your company has published about the problems you solve, product market fit, company mission and key messaging. Find a newsletter, learn the jargon and hunt down every single three letter acronym. Re-read your company's white papers. If there's science behind what you do, read some of the technical content that backs up what marketing publishes.

After you've read everything the company has published, go talk to a couple people a couple of rungs up the ladder in your org. Go to your boss's boss in Sales, or ask a senior product manager, or even the VP and say the following:

> *"I'm trying to nail my POV of what we do for our customers' problems. Can I buy you lunch?"*

Every one of these folks already has a POV, even if it's informal. You'll get a true expert, original-source perspective that you can incorporate into your own way of talking about the problems you solve.

At the same time you'll be recognized as a curious and self-starting human who wants to serve customers and the company better. Those are the exact traits leaders look for when they're thinking about promotions.

Finally, there is zero chance that that leader will let you buy, so you get a free lunch.

2. Write it down

Your inventory research probably didn't deliver a nice clean summary called "My POV". So you have to make one yourself.

Ideally this whole thing is no more than two pages.

Define your urgent and important problem
In your own words, write down the problem you solve and describe how the customer would determine that this problem is important.

Buyer:	Who is your ideal customer?
Objective:	What job do they want to do?
Problem:	What is stopping them doing this?
Importance:	How does this cost them money or expose them to risk?
Urgency:	How bad can the problem get within how much time?

Take your time on this, it's harder than it seems.

Dig down three levels of "Why" to find the root causes of that problem.

Understanding the root cause of the problems you solve for is at the center of your entire POV. What does the problem look like from the outside? What's the underlying reason? What's the reason for that reason?

The first level of "why" is something the buyer would probably already know. You just need to show you know it too.

The second level "why" they may or may not already know. This is where your industry or role knowledge kicks in. Your competitors (or anyone who spends a lot of time thinking about this space) would probably agree with your assessment.

The third level down is your company's secret sauce. An insight that only you have about the problem. This is not your tech or your product, though it might be what your tech is based on.

It doesn't have to be hard science, it could simply be that your company has assembled a unique data set or you've accumulated significant time specialized on the job and you've learned some stuff that lets you do what you do better than anyone else.

One note: the root cause is never "because you didn't buy our software".

Ultimately we want enough of an insight into the root cause such that, in principle, a determined person who hears your breakdown could fix their problem from scratch. Going it alone might not be cost effective, or they may not have the tools or assets to create a solution in a reasonable amount of time, but they'd understand how it *could* be done.

You'll use this deep knowledge early on to demonstrate credibility, then again later when you're figuring out the value your solution has to a specific customer… so you know what to charge them.

Write down the symptoms

Once you understand the root causes of the problem, go downstream a little and think about how to connect what you know to what your buyers care about. That might not be the problem itself. More likely, they're only aware of symptoms.

So what are some symptoms that might indicate someone has ventured into your domain of expertise? What search terms would someone type when trying to figure out how to fix the problem you fix?

Sketch out the mechanics of how your company's solution works
You're not writing down your proprietary algorithms or the exact 11 herbs and spices, but rather capturing the workflow of how your product does its thing. Imagine a whiteboard with a flow chart showing the business process of your customers. Circle the parts that are broken. Draw arrows to show where your solution intervenes and makes a change. What is that change? Now that the business process is no longer broken, what's different?

Those are the mechanics of your solution.

This is a really powerful moment for your POV. You now have a chain of understanding from symptom to problem to root cause to solution. You'll suddenly see clear as day the value that you're creating for your customer. And you'll see red flags too. Did your "fixes" add a bunch of work for your customer (or maybe one team) in return for an improvement that's hard to quantify? You'll have to think about how to handle that in your sales pitch.

Before you know it, you'll be connecting dots between different news items, predicting the conclusion of articles based on the first couple paragraphs and jumping in and out of conversations at any level with confidence and ease, meeting each buyer wherever they're at.

In other words, you have a POV.

SLIGHTLY MORE EFFICIENT SELLING

3. Wordsmith your POV

The key to a great point of view is that it's your language and you're comfortable talking about it. You might think you get points for trying, but if you come across as someone who's just reciting things they don't really understand, it just reminds your customer that you're not the trusted expert they're looking for.

There's an easy fix: practice.

☐ Even if you're not accustomed to prospecting, send out some cold emails based around your POV and see if they land. Call a recently-won friendly customer and ask if you can try some new language with them.

☐ Test a couple different ways of phrasing the symptoms, search the web to see if other people (a) talk about the problems the same way you do and (b) are already offering the insights that you think only you know.

☐ Wait a week and go look at your language. Try something different and send that out too.

You'll change this 100 times over the next six months, and a year from now you'll think "how on earth did I think this was good?"

That self-awareness is actually fantastic. It means you're still learning and growing.

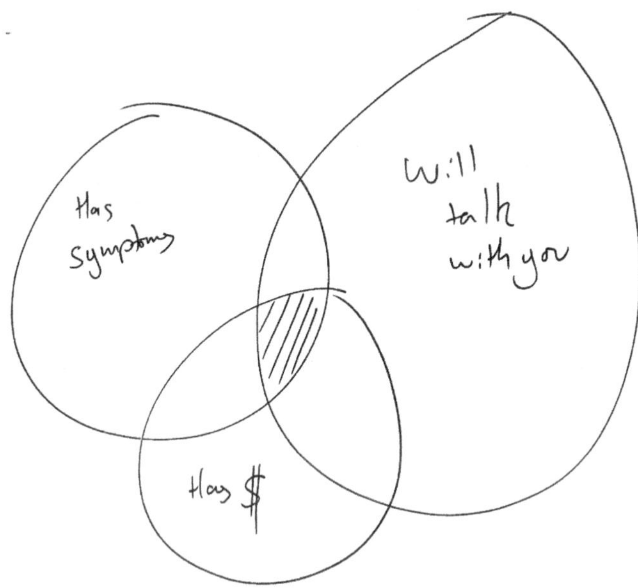

CHAPTER 3 | Prospecting

Finding people with urgent important problems you can fix

You can always get a meeting by being charming / persistent/ funny or talking about their football team, but to get a meeting with someone who will actually buy, you need to find someone with the problem you fix.

They probably don't know they have the problem, so you're looking for people with the symptoms. People who are also willing to collaborate to see if it's a UIP that can be fixed. And who have money to give to you. And access to power. And bandwidth to go the whole mile figuring it all out.

It's easy to see how you can burn through names real fast. And we didn't even say "AI" yet.

Most sales orgs think of lead generation in terms of Inbound, where Marketing creates interest from content or webinars etc., and Outbound activities like cold calling and cold emailing.

Reluctant to place their livelihoods in the hands of others, smart sellers treat their current customers as their best source of new opportunities, both in terms of expansions and referrals.

These all have their place, and we'll take a quick survey of the options below to get the meeting, but I'm more interested in what you do in that first call to connect with the customer and help you both understand if they have an urgent and important problem you can help them fix.

Inbound

As an individual seller, you're going to have a really hard time creating successful inbound. The closest you can get is social selling, where you can repackage Marketing's content and broadcast it to your network.

So the question is more about how to handle a lead that comes to you from Marketing.

First and foremost is speed. I spent two mins looking this up on the internet. Harvard Business Review claims you decrease your odds by 400% if response time slips from 5 to 10 minutes.

That's crazy.

The challenge is that during those precious 5 minutes, you need to study up, because the kudos of a fast answer is totally negated if you show up knowing nothing about the company or their problem.

5 Min Speed Study

First 90 seconds — Look at the company's website. Categorize their business and load up any current customers in the same business into your brain. Be like a method actor and pretend you work there. Look at their customer logos to get a sense if this is an established company catering to well known brands or a startup. Personally I'm also judging their marketing team's design chops to figure out if they have money.

Min 1.5 to Min 3 — Look up the person's LinkedIn. Read any posts they posted or commented on. This will give you a hint to what they care about. If you're really lucky, you can weave what they said into your conversation. If you're a horrible, shallow person like myself, you can look at their photo to judge whether they're going to be friendly. If you do do this, prepare to be wrong approximately 50% of the time.

Min 3 to 3:30 — Look at the company's LinkedIn and TechCrunch. You're just looking to see if they've got money, if they've posted any news. Look on the company's People page to see if you know anyone and if they're hiring (that's a good sign for you).

Min 3:30 to 5 — Clear your mind, and apply your POV to what you just learned about their company. What urgent and important problems might they have, and what symptoms of those problems might they be experiencing? If you worked there and you knew what you know from your POV, what would you worried about? What would you be doing to fix it?

OK! Write down a couple bullet points and you're ready. Just be aware that Inbound people might be further along the Education phase than someone you hooked cold via Outbound…

Outbound

As an individual contributor, you need to do your own outbound prospecting. Cold outbound will keep you sharp and let you practice your POV so many times it'll truly become second nature. There's also a strong chance that thanks to AI, the SDR model becomes economically unviable and you have no choice but to fend for yourself.

So how do you find people who will listen as you say "I think you have an urgent and important problem and I have the solution" in 10 seconds?

Before AI, you built a list (or were given a list) based on an ideal customer profile. You were told to do your research, in the hope you'd find prospects begging for your product who for some reason hadn't bothered to call you. You looked on LinkedIn, trade websites, job postings, company blogs for nuggets you could use to connect with the prospect: a blog post, a news item, their favorite team.

You probably don't find anything. That's why cold calling has such a low success rate.

It worked because automated outbounding tools like Groove and Outreach made it easy to email so many thousands of people with your pitch that even 0.1% success was good enough. Maybe the first email was personalized, but the second through 5th touch were just bumps.

Here in 2024, AI companies like copy.ai promise customized emails at scale. The problem is when everyone (including your competitors) uses these tools, the amount of low-quality-but-okay email will drown out any chance for even the best crafted and perfectly customized cold email.

So what's ado?

For cold outbound, I think most sellers will enter the arms race and use AI to send out massive quantities of low-quality-but-okay emails hoping to break through. I think SDRs will fade away because (a) the AI can write just about the same quality email as a junior seller, (b) all that AI email will make the yields even worse than they are today and (c) the end of zero interest percentage rates means companies can't just afford the bodies. I think sellers will be forced to pick up the phone, pay for dialers, pay for cell phone numbers, add texting to their automated cadences and more til this channel is oversaturated too.

Slightly more efficient sellers will do something different.

All of the above means you can't just send short notes saying you've helped similar companies and ask for a demo. You need to be actually helpful.

You have a POV. You know something they don't know about an urgent and important problem that they might have. You could save their jobs. You also have plenty of time and a bunch of machines that will do work for you. So tell them what you know they should know.

Put some of that POV, the deep stuff, into a cadence and drip it. Add some of that personal stuff about sports and college if your data shows it helps. But focus on giving real actual counsel based on what you know.

Send your second and third level root causes. Tell them you're a slightly more efficient seller and you believe that together you can both make some money by fixing an efficiency and that it's easier to work with you, but you'll show them how to do it themselves. Be genuine and actually want to help.

But with all that trash out there, it's still going to be horrible.

I'd be spending a lot more time working on referrals and keeping my network strong.

———

Referrals

Referrals are where it's at. Free trust and credibility.

While an Account Manager is in a better position to ask for a referral, all is not lost.

Every top seller knows that the end of the deal is not at Closed. Or even Go Live. The real end of the deal is the moment when the customer sees value and is glad that they put their neck out to choose you over the other vendor or going the DIY route.

As a seller, your whole sales motion should be beady-eye on that day, what I like to call "Thank God I Gave You Money Day". Even after you've handed over the deal to implementation and the customer success team, keep in contact with your customer. And when you think it's close to TGIGYMD, go for the ask.

1. Did we deliver as promised?
2. Do you think any of [these other companies] would see the same gains?
3. Can you intro me?

Make sure for (2) that you've got a well-researched list — people with the problems you fix who could/should/might want to get that problem fixed… and who could/should/might have the money to work with you.

Referrals are gold, but you're asking a lot, so you've got to be tight in your ask, and it's all about the timing of them feeling good and grateful on TGIGYMD.

Your first 30 min call

OK. You secured the meetings. What do you say?

Most companies will provide a "first call deck" courtesy of Marketing. But I want you to ask yourself if a polished actor presenting that first call deck would make a great video.

If the answer is yes, it's a terrible first call deck.

So many selling orgs treat their First Call like an ad for their company. "We've served 2000 customers. Our software can do so much. Our customers save $1M just by using our software."

That's not your job. That's Marketing's job. And I promise your customer doesn't believe you. In fact they're not even really listening.

Remember the goals of being Slightly More Efficient from the intro?

1. Does the customer have a problem that is urgent and important?
2. Can you solve the problem faster or more reliably than they could do it themselves?
3. Can you convince the customer that the first two things are true?

Before we get into root cause, or case studies or demos or costs or anything, let's figure out if they actually have a problem and make sure they understand you might be able to help them.

You learn you can't help them? Great! You're being slightly more efficient with everyone's time.

The conflict though is that in your prospect's mind, the most efficient path is for you to show them your stuff so they can decide real quick if it solves a problem they have.

Giving them that demo with zero context is the lazy way out. It's easy in the moment, but long term, you'll both end up worse off.

Your job is to convince the customer that you know something about a problem they may have, and that problem is urgent and important. You need to convince them that it's worth the time to learn more about this problem and that it's fixable.

Even if the prospect knows about their problem, they still need to know that you know the problem too. They still need context for what you're going to show them, and you need info from them too. So hold strong and don't jump to demo too fast.

Let's imagine that you've won a 30 minute call with a buyer. Maybe it was 100% cold, maybe it was a referral. However it came to be, you've done a little bit of research and you think this person might have the problem you solve.

Following is what a first call might look like.

Minute by Minute Call Breakdown

Intros & Your Promise (5 mins)

" I swear to God I will do a demo of my stuff in this call so you know I'm not wasting your time. By the time we're done, you'll know a little bit more about [the urgent important problem], how you might think about calculating cost of fixing vs. leaving it alone, and how you might fix it if it's worth fixing. What I want out of this call is to share what I know to make the world a slightly better place and hear your feedback, because then I'll know if we can help or if you're gonna take it on yourself. I also want to make sure we leave 10 mins at the end for a fly through demo and next steps.

What do you want to get out of this call?"

Main Body (15 mins)

1. Hook them with a symptom they have to show you spent some time learning about them. Ask about the cost of the underlying problem and what they're doing about it.
2. Show your POV and un-peel one level of Root Cause that causes the symptom.
3. Ask them about other symptoms that are also causing pain.
4. Show them a 5 min demo of a fixed future (you're painting a picture here of their life being better when using your solution, NOT a feature tour).

Next Steps (10 mins)

5. Take questions about their pain and your POV, but be firm about no more demo.
    1. Yes it can → Why do you ask?
    2. Happy to show you when we meet → Let's set that time (ideally in less than a week)
6. If they broadly agree about the urgent and important problem and recognize you have the chops to help and they're interested in hearing more of your insights: Success!

A couple notes

• This is not a script. You need to take the ideas and use your own words.

• Assuming this is an online meeting, do this with as little screen share as possible. It's really important that they can see your face. If you have to screen share, then share and close, share and close, so most of the time it's full face.

• Be hardcore about talk / listen ratios. I strive for me talking 42% and them talking 58%.

• The hardest part is a 5 min demo. Show a slide of how your solution works and all the things you *could* demo, but limit yourself to one single path for the actual demo. You're just proving your software is real here not giving a training.

Yes I agree: I (may) have an urgent and important problem

How many sales books have you read where they say it's that easy?

It's never going to go like this. They're going to say "no, you called me, just give the demo" or they're going to ask for pricing. In reality, every new call is going to be a compromise.

It might take more than one call for the customer to acknowledge they have (or may have) an urgent and important problem. You might need more than one buyer on that call, and you might end up doing this call a couple times with different people.

 SLIGHTLY MORE EFFICIENT SELLING

Remember, you don't need to quantify or even prove there's problem at this point; that'll come when you're evaluating the "Do nothing" option in the second phase.

Be cool, focus on being slightly more efficient, show them you really want to help, and try to forget about quota retirement for a minute.

It will pay you back in no time.

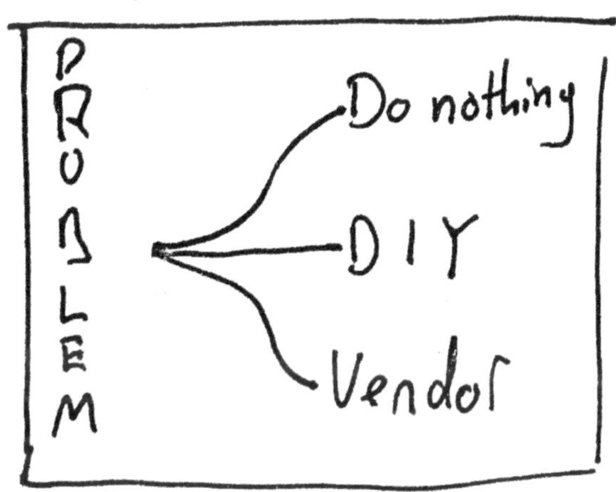

CHAPTER 4 | The Fix

Do Nothing, DIY or Get a Vendor

Now that your prospect understands they (may) have an Urgent and Important Problem, you need to help them understand their options to fix it. A lot of reps make a massive mistake right here by jumping straight to "buy my stuff", but you can avoid this killer error in 2 mins at the top of your education phase.

Right out of the gate, acknowledge the facts. Say there are exactly three things you can do with a problem: Do nothing, fix it yourself or find a vendor. Say you're here to share what you know and help them make that decision.

They already know they have this choice. So own it.

Explaining your game plan will reset expectations about who you are and why you're different than all the other sellers out there. You're also getting their commitment to share with you.

You already introduced this framework in your 30 minute intro, but you need to call it out explicitly. You don't need slides. Just say the below in your own words. Should take 60 seconds.

How I propose we do business together

1. *We'll discuss the nature of your problem and possible root causes. If we agree there is a problem, then we'll advance to step 2. If not, we'll part as friends.*

2. *We'll discuss and agree that for any problem in the world, there are three and only three options: Do nothing, do it yourself or pay a vendor.*

3. *We'll look at all three options together with a rational evaluation of the costs, risks and benefits of each approach, and you (the buyer) will decide what's best for you. If it's "do nothing" or DIY, we part as trusted friends who have shared something special together.*

4. *If this all sounds right and you (the buyer) decide "pay a vendor" is the right choice, we'll both bring the right people to the table to make the final decision.*

This is the core of Slightly More Efficient — forcing the decision making process into the open, showing your hand early, acknowledging your own interests, and actually helping.

You already covered most or even all of #1 in your first prospecting call. If we set aside government bailouts or a cooperative barn raising, then #2 should be an instant agreement. For #3, it's totally ok to acknowledge that you're hoping for "Pay a vendor", but say you're designing the process so it's super transparent, and recommit that ultimately your goal is to give your prospect what they need to make their decision.

For #4, you're setting an expectation that once your champion understands their options and is leaning towards a vendor, you'll be sharing the lessons up the ladder together. A mutual action plan is fantastic for establishing this kind of expectation and holding your champion accountable later.

If you've done a good job of explaining the problem, you should have no problem getting a second meeting with more senior decision makers. You want to position that second meeting with your champion leading the explanation, and you're just there as backup. Let your champion be the main bearer of insights, but make sure you're in the room so everyone else bears witness to the originator of those insights.

Finally, commit to giving a worksheet to your prospect to track the pros and cons of each approach. That way they own the inputs and the outputs of their decision-making process that will go on to create your mutual business case.

The nature of the problem & possible root causes

Would you rather go to a doctor who doesn't really know why the medicine works, or one who understands the mechanism of the drug interactions with your personal chemistry?

Fixing symptoms is always a temporary answer. Whether it's your body or a business, you need to fix the root cause of problems.

As a seller, the primary reason you want to get into the root cause is because it shows you're a much safer choice than DIY or choosing another vendor: you want to be seen as the low risk option.

You have to come in at this point with a couple ounces of self-awareness.

Yes, you have your POV that knows something they don't know. Yes, it's been proven successful at other companies. But no two situations are always exactly alike. And even if they are pretty similar, nobody likes being told they're exactly the same as everyone else.

At this point in the relationship, you literally know just enough to be dangerous. You have to listen more than you talk, and be real careful that you don't make assumptions as you brashly squeeze the customer in front of you into a predefined box of your own making.

At the same time, have faith in your POV. It's got you this far. Based on what you know, you should be able to predict multiple levels of symptoms because you know where to look. The equivalent of the doctor asking "does it hurt here?"

The idea is that by predicting some of their symptoms — especially ones they don't know about themselves until you tell them where to look — they'll want to listen, because you've shown you know something worth knowing.

So take your time and explain the problem to them, and show them what's really happening.

This requires some risk on your behalf, because you're not showing off software. You're teaching them why their business isn't working right. That's normally the job of a consultant paid hundreds of thousands. And here you are giving away this info freely, knowing that they might take your insights and try to DIY a solution. You're giving it away knowing they'll use your know-how to shop for cheaper vendors.

But that risk is what sets you apart from everyone else. It's what makes you genuinely, actually helpful and valuable, rather than just paying lip service to being customer centric.

And assuming your product or solution has some value add beyond just knowing the problem space, you're still pretty safe.

SLIGHTLY MORE EFFICIENT SELLING

Remember: this part of the process still has exactly ZERO to do with your product, but there is a caveat. As a buyer, it takes a ton of faith, and not a small amount of humility to listen to a seller explain your business problems back to you.

Your buyer's natural inclination will be to say "yeah, got it, show me the software".

Recognize their very reasonable impatience here, and transition from Root Cause to Fix by asking a simple question

"OK. Given what I just showed you about the root cause, how would you DIY the solution?"

Until you understand how they'd DIY, it's going to be hard to sell them anything anyway, so stay strong and dig into the DIY with them.

Figure out the fix

Before we go on, I hope your product fixes the root cause of the problem you've uncovered. But if during this next phase you find out it's not going to for this customer, then get out now.

There's honor and value in saying "this isn't for us". You'll save yourself time, you'll bank some SME karma, and your prospect will remember you as a knowledgeable, ethical, helpful expert next time they have a problem. Yes, you're a hungry, disappointed expert who's gonna miss your number, but you can't have it all.

But most of the time, if your POV has any actual insight, you'll have got to the point where the champion and their senior decision maker understands there's a real urgent important problem. And that problem has a root cause that you were able to explain to them in a way that they understood.

They're primed for the fix.

But don't jump just yet. You need to answer two big questions.

1.   What is the cost of doing nothing?
2.   What's the cost of just fixing it in-house?

As a seller, you need to know these numbers, because this is your real competition, and your buyer is going to come up with these numbers with or without you. So choose "with you" and have a chance at influencing the outcome with your experience and insights.

This is the centerpiece of being Slightly More Efficient. Over on the buying side of this book it's all that I talk about. So pay attention:

The DIHAP Worksheet — Do I Have a Problem

When you laid out your process, you promised to include all three options available to address a problem: Do nothing, DIY or pay a vendor. You have to do this in a spreadsheet, and your customer needs to own the inputs. The math needs to be simple. And no sneaky multipliers.

	DO NOTHING	DIY	VENDOR
Cost of change			
Opportunity cost of effort			
Benefit of change			
NET OUTCOME			

Option 1 Do Nothing

The cost of Do Nothing is equal to the cost of the urgent and important problem. By pricing it out as one of three viable paths, you're highlighting that fact that losing money to a problem is exactly the same as spending money. But a problem can cost in lots of different ways, so make sure you account for all of them.

How does this problem cost money?

1. **Actual money** — This is the easiest on paper, but often a challenge to prove. The oil pipe is old and when it ruptures then $3M of oil will be lost, plus the $5M in cleanup costs. It's only useful if everyone agrees the pipe is definitely going to rupture. There are more important, larger costs to be considered before doing nothing.

2. **Risk** — If the problem is just a case of adding risk (like risk of a lawsuit or compliance order from the government) you can quantify this by taking the cost of the bad thing times the percent chance of it happening. You'll need your champion to help here, but you should have a good guess if you did your POV homework.

3. **Employee time** — If the problem is wasting employee time, it's a little trickier. Unless you think your customer is going to furlough employees for a few hours every week, I don't think people are ever convinced by employee-salary-cost-per-hour arguments. You might have a better case if your champion can tell you what the value of a productive hour is — 10 sales calls, 20 widgets off a production line?

Before you're done here, you need to make this cost real, so be sure to include a time component.

What is the cost of Doing Nothing for a month? A year?

Will the cost-per-month change for the better or worse over time?

Is there a spike that's coming? How do you know?

They've already been doing nothing for a while now. How much has that cost them since the problem started?

	DO NOTHING	DIY	VENDOR
Cost of change			
Opportunity cost of effort			
Benefit of change			
NET OUTCOME			

SLIGHTLY MORE EFFICIENT SELLING

Option 2 DIY

You got your customer's forbearance to spend time on this root cause stuff in return for a promise that they might be able to fix this problem on their own. So let's cover that next.

"OK. Given what we understand about the root cause, how could you DIY the solution?"

This reassures them that they still have DIY open as an option, but for you it's your chance to validate that your root cause analysis is right. You can start doing discovery around the change management that's going to be needed for implementing the solution (whether that be theirs or yours) plus the cost and risks they'd have to incur if they go the DIY route. You'll need all this data when you're putting together the evaluation of which route they should take.

Part of your POV needs to include an "analog" or manual version of your solution. What is it actually doing under the hood? If they wanted to replicate it, how would they do it? Be confident in your competitive moat and tell them all the things.

Spell it out in the spreadsheet and let them put in their own numbers for what it'll take for them to provision all the things. Be comprehensive, but keep it honest. If they catch you being disingenuous here, you'll lose the deal. You want to give enough detail to paint a convincing picture of what it would take for them to do this themselves.

Think of it as listing what questions need to asked rather than giving them the answer key to the test. Of course, you're not going to give away any IP or trade secrets.

Here's a starter list for the questions they need to answer. Note that a lot of this is overhead unrelated to the actual fix, but it's necessary if they want to build and support a solution in-house.

Checklist Questions

You can use your own company's product as a starting point to help model the effort in creating a fix, but essentially you're asking the buyer to think through all the effort DIY will really take.

- How long will the design phase take?
- Who has the expertise in-house to validate the design?
- How many people will this project take away from their day jobs? Can they be spared? Do they all know what they're doing? Will they want to help?
- What other teams will need to be consulted or do work?
- Where will this fall on their priority list?
- What could go wrong? What are the costs if something goes slightly wrong? Very wrong?
- What are the ongoing costs 3 months, 6 months, a year later?
- Don't forget the ancillary stuff like user onboarding & support, documentation, keeping dependencies up to date, upgrades, triage, feature requests

Your goal in listing all this stuff is for the buyer to make a real, rational decision on the true cost of trying to do this by themselves. You're not showing them how to do it, just listing all the topics they need to take onboard and figure out.

"I can just do it with a spreadsheet"

There's a good chance that your buyer thinks they can make do with a spreadsheet. But spreadsheets break down when they go from proof-of-concept to mission-critical production.

- Do you have safety checks to make sure all the connections are working?
- Who has write access to the sheet? How can you know they don't mess with your formulas?
- Are the connectors to other datasources (spreadsheets, databases, other services) reliant on a specific user's credentials? What happens if that person leaves or logs out?
- Is the spreadsheet set up for long term use, are there limits on data or row count etc?
- How do you manage sync control issues?

SLIGHTLY MORE EFFICIENT SELLING

"We're a software company, our engineers will just build an internal app"

Every engineering team thinks they can build any software. And they might be able to spike a first proof of concept. But that last 80% is tough.

- **Security** — No one wants to be the person who exposed their company to liability or data breach. Does your app touch the internet or have any external users or use any third party libraries? If yes, you'll need to design with security in mind from the first.

- **User management** — Will you have users logging in? Will you connect to an existing directory or authentication system? Managing users will become a full-time job.

- **Upgrades & feature enhancement** — No product is ever final in v1. Ironically, the more successful your app is, the more feature improvement requests you'll get that you'll need to handle.

- **Library & dependencies support** — Are you using any open source libraries or other dependencies? Think TinyMCE for form inputs. How are you going to know updates are necessary or when a dependencies has a security breach?

By the time you've walked your buyer through these questions, you should have a tab on your spreadsheet summarizing what your buyer would do to solve the problem:

1. How they would approach the fix
2. How much it would cost in actual dollars
3. The amount of effort to build the fix
4. The amount of effort to rollout and maintain
5. Who would be doing this, and what's the commitment level & timeline
6. What are the risk factors?
7. What are the costs if things go wrong, and who bears those costs?

This might require some work the first time during your first POV prep, but it's going to be pretty consistent, and customers will appreciate your template and will probably go with the numbers you suggest as long as they're even close to reasonable.

Take those numbers and put them in a new column next to Do Nothing.

	DO NOTHING	DIY	VENDOR
Cost of change			
Opportunity cost of effort			
Benefit of change			
NET OUTCOME			

But this is only the first part of the cost equation of DIY.

The real cost comes from time and risk.

The whole period that they're prepping their DIY - decision, design, build, implement, fail, redesign, rebuild, implement again — the urgent important problem is ticking along costing money.

The time of the people doing the DIY has an opportunity cost. What project or what part of running the business was neglected while folks jumped in to fix this problem?

Then even when it's done, there's near 100% certainty that the fix will never be as successful in fixing the problem as having the pros doing it.

And there's a not-insubstantial risk that the DIY project totally fails, and the buyer is now six months deeper into the problem, way behind on their other projects, burnt a ton of political capital and is now in a much worse negotiating position when talking to vendors.

Put that in the spreadsheet too.

Option 3 Pay a Vendor

You've been so patient. You worked through do nothing and DIY like a trooper. You did it to earn trust and credibility, but you also learned what you need to know to make an ironclad business case. So now, if you did everything right, the customer is thinking

> *"Hmm. Do Nothing would be very costly to ignore. I could build it in-house, but quite a lot of effort and rather risky. I see that now. I should consider this go-with-a-vendor option."*

You need to connect the final dot. Yes. It's demo time.

But no, it's not that easy. While you're showing how you fix the problem, you need to bake in how much less effort and how much less risky it is to fix the problem with you rather than them going DIY.

1. Show you fix the problem with your solution

This is old hat to you. Your good ol' demo. The only thing you could do wrong now is do a left-to-right "harbor tour" of your product instead of showing it fixing the prospect's problem.

You want to frame your demo in the terms of the symptoms that you've been referring to this whole time, so ideally you can use your prospect's data / situation or something close to it rather than a generic demo environment. The less they have to imagine, the easier your job will be to show them your solution is safe and realistic and will actually deliver.

Run through the process of using your stuff to fix their problem. Call out what you're doing as if you were an employee at their company and show how those symptoms go away because you're fixing that root cause you talked about.

If they ask to dive into the details, it's reasonable go down the rabbit hole a little bit, if just to show your software is real, but if they want to dig a lot deeper, push back politely and ask why they want to know. They won't say "because I don't trust you" but if that's the sense you're getting, then address it head on and ask "is there something you're having a hard time with?"

You need to figure out if they're having trouble with your POV / general approach or if it's something more practical like UI or license.

Chances are it's an assumption you made in your POV.

I'll give an example from my own company DealPoint. We made mutual action plan software. Easily the most common concern we faced in early discovery was "I don't think customers will use it". That's not a question that any number of software demos will answer. But when we showed usage stats and offered calls with other customers, we were able to move forward.

The thing is sometimes it took a little coaxing to get them to say it because they didn't want to be rude. So in our case, we started building in those proof points early in our POV so we could preempt the objection.

If it's a more technical question or if they're just curious, then promise you'll go as deep as they want, but suggest you confirm that your solution will fix their problem first. Because if it's not going to work in general, then there's no point wasting time in the details.

You want to get to the stage where the customer says "If everything you say is true about your solution, then yes, it would fix my problem."

Then you can go on to the next step, which is showing that your approach is better than DIY.

2. Show that "Pay a Vendor" is better / faster / less risky than DIY

Assuming the cost of Do Nothing is too high to ignore, your buyer now has two viable options: DIY or Vendor.

DIY may be cheaper in terms of hard costs, but your job is to draw a direct comparison between the two across three other variables: effectiveness of the fix, time to implement and risk.

We're going to put all those concerns you described during the DIY evaluation on a timeline comparing the two approaches. This could be done in the same spreadsheet or you can make it look nicer on a slide.

- **Effectiveness** — It's a given that a DIY version of anything isn't going to be as effective as a professionally developed version. How can you work out what percent less effective?

- **Time to implement** — On the Vendor side of the timeline, there's zero development time of course so you're already way ahead of the game. But development is only the beginning. Contrast implementation time for each of the items you listed in the DIY checklist. Include call-outs for the effort required of other teams.

- **Risk** — Show the risk spots in the DIY approach where things can go off the rails. Development could run long, version one might be deemed too hard to use or turn out to be missing something critical.

You don't want to risk your credibility here, so be fair and transparent in your comparisons.

If you have a good product, you should come out favorably, and anyone looking at this slide will say "That DIY approach looks higher risk and seems like it takes longer too"

3. Change management will be your prospect's biggest concern, so don't undersell it

Show them you have a well defined plan of action that will get them from here to there over a series of safe, knowable, zero-risk milestones.

Keep their confidence by showing how each of those milestones has its own success criteria to prove you're on the right path.

Mutual action plans are fantastic for this.

4. Share pricing, but present it as a range

You have to share pricing at this point. You've looked at the cost of doing nothing. You've looked at the non-tangibles of DIY. All else being equal, of course they'd go with a vendor. But it's not all equal because going with a vendor takes money. So before they can go too far down the path with you, they need to know how much money might be required.

The key here is to provide a range. Some less ethical sellers might try and anchor on a high price, but I already told the buyers about this trick over on the buyer Side. So share reasonable pricing.

It's also appropriate here to show what levers you have available that impact which end of the range they'll end up at. You don't need to show the exact math, just explain "here's the range $X to $Y, with the levers of volume, time, signing date, marketing available as give-to-gets.

A final note about competition

A competitor could appear at any stage in this process. But the Slightly More Efficient principles hold the same no matter who's on the stage.

No buyer buys on price alone. Trust, capability, and credibility are all huge competitive moats.

Showing you understand the root causes, and showing you're willing to share your expertise as your buyer dives deep into No Nothing and DIY will lock out any competitor.

So stand strong and keep being helpful. The competition — with their price sheet, gormless grin, and total ignorance of why their solution works — will be left by the wayside every time.

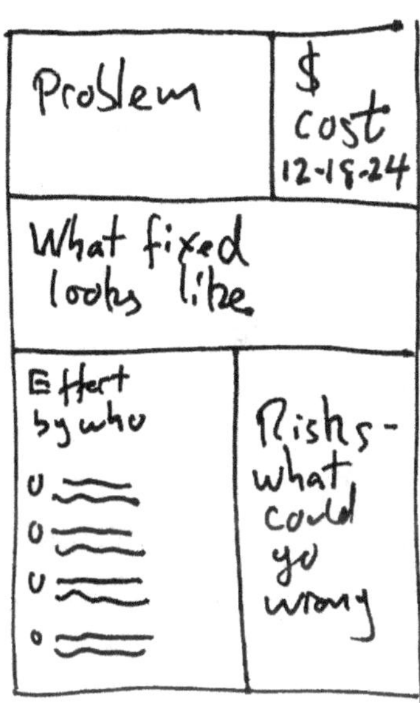

CHAPTER 5 | Getting To Yes

From "I want your solution" to "We want to buy your solution"

So far so good. But we haven't actually proven anything yet. It's all still in principle. More important for sellers, your Champion could agree with absolutely every checklist item so far, they could really really want your solution and firmly believe it's the best choice over Do nothing and DIY, and they're still not going to buy.

To get to yes, you need to prove value beyond any financial doubt, you need to show a safe path to make it happen and you need to do it to the satisfaction of the people who hold the power.

Proof of Concept (aka Proof of Value)

"Proof of Concept" and "Proof of Value" are nearly interchangeable. I'm going with "POC" since I already use POV for Point of View all over the place and I don't want to get us both confused.

At this stage in your buyer's decision making process, they're on the fence. They've grown to trust you enough to listen. Everything you've said so far has checked out as true, but despite all the facts, "do nothing" is still really tempting.

The go-to offer is "try it for yourself". But designing a trial that actually proves your case is really hard. Neither side is fully committed, so you're never going to get the results you'd see if everyone was properly engaged. Trials also take time and effort, which is the antithesis of being slightly more efficient.

The gold standard is a reference customer in the same industry/circumstance as your buyer standing up and saying "I was in the same pain-boat as you are now. I bought the thing, and now I'm no longer in the pain-boat."

But reference customers are a precious commodity with a limited number of times you can call on them.

So what's left?

1. The trusty Case Study

Best for the seller is the honorable case study. You don't have to bother your current customers, and case studies can be consumed at the buyer's convenience.

The problem is there have been so many terrible case studies, or even outright frauds, that buyers have every right to be skeptical. Plus your current customer is unlikely to let you publish their actual numbers, either the cost of the pain you fixed, or the incredible health of their new golden world.

You can make your case study more credible in a couple ways. Although really, this is a job for your marketing department. So rip out this page of the book and give it to marketing.

In no more than two sides of a page, outline the specifics of the problem that your case study customer was experiencing and then show you delivered on the promise to fix it.

1. Summarize the pain and solution in 50 words or less. That is probably all the current prospect is going to read.

2. Build a quote that focuses on the pain and the good place they're now at. Ideally you can construct this from snippets of actual quote so it's easy for your champion to approve. Make that quote real big on the page.

3. Try to get your customer to agree to share the numbers from your "Do I Have a Problem" (or DIHAP) worksheet, but recognize they probably won't let you.

4. Don't downplay change management. Have a section that specifically calls out how long implementation took and see if you can get someone to say it was smooth. This quote should be on the back page, so you have a pull-quote on both sides of the case study.

5. Even though it's called a case study and is ostensibly about a single customer, include your typical improvement metrics, ideally showing a couple of different customer sizes so your current prospect can see themselves in the stats.

6. Make sure that your org does all the work. The only thing the customers should have to do is approve the whole thing. But be respectful. Position it as "a starter" or "a draft" so they don't think you're too assumptive.

2. The reliable Reference Customer

As a seller, you'll have more control over reference customers than you will with case studies (which are typically the domain of Marketing). Finding those references can be super simple: just ask your favorite customers if they'd take a phone call. Nothing in writing, no big deal.

In this quasi "off the record" approach, your reference customer is more likely to share their experiences, and it definitely requires less approval than a printed quote.

The risk is you'll never know for sure what they'll say. So ask. Position it as a quick prep for your reference customers along the lines of "here's some of the things a potential buyer may ask". It'll be great feedback for you, your customer will feel listened to, and you'll have more confidence in their response.

If you're maintaining your own references (rather than relying on Marketing's approved people) be aware that there are only so many times you can ask a customer to take a call. This is yet another reason why the best sellers stay in contact with their customers long after the sale. If you keep in touch and continue giving value, they're a lot more likely to help you out with a reference call, and over time you're a lot more likely to have a lot more people to tap.

Track who you've asked and when you last made a request to each person so you don't burn them out. Don't forget to say thank you after.

3. The dreaded Pilot

If a case study and a reference customer don't deliver sufficient proof in the eyes of your buyer, it's probably because you don't have great case studies and reference customers. Make a note and tell marketing they're letting you down and making your job harder.

If the buyer is only going to accept a pilot or trial, you need to construct it really carefully otherwise you're going to (a) fail to prove your point and (b) give away a TON of value that's going to be hard to recoup later.

What are you proving?

It's important to start with the right goal. Just proving your product works isn't enough to make them buy. You need to prove you can fix their problem. That means you need to over-index on the approach — how your solution is going to fix their problem, what change management needs to look like. Then sure, show that the software actually works too.

When scientists want to test something, they don't test the whole system. They get a test tube and design the smallest test possible that proves the principle. That's what you need to do. It doesn't necessarily need to mimic a real deployment. You just need to prove your approach to fixing their problem will work.

To design that small test, you need to think about a few things:

1. **What *is* the approach?**
    It can't just be "buy my software". You need to write down what change they're going to see after buying your solution. Ideally you already did this when talking about what Fixed looks like, so this should be easy.

2. **What might go wrong?**
    You're testing your approach. Where are the risky moments? This HAS to come from your

customer. Where do they think it's going to go bad? User rollout and adoption? Integration into their existing tech? Moving data from the old system into yours? Ensuring continuity of results? Your solution actually working right is almost certainly NOT on their list. Once you've identified the risk vectors, how are you designing guardrails to make sure those risks don't happen?

3. **What's the shortest amount of time this test tube needs to sit?**
   Remember, you don't need to prove your whole value prop to the nth degree. Just enough to show it's safer than Do Nothing or DIY.

4. **How will you and the buyer know your pilot was a success?**
   Do you have a metric you can measure? Most pilots don't. So whose thumbs up suffices in lieu of hard numbers? What is that person looking for? Get that in writing before you start to stop the line shifting. It's gonna shift anyway, but do what you can.

Once you've designed the pilot, you need to make sure it runs REAL smooth.

1. **Pick the teams mindfully**
   Your natural inclination is to cherry pick the pilot team, but while that stacks the odds in your favor for a good pilot, it also creates an escape route for a skeptical buyer to say "yeah, those results were with our best people. They'd do great even if they only had a couple rocks to bang together."

   So instead, ask for two teams: one stellar team to demonstrate the amazing potential of your approach with top performers, and one average team to prove that your solution can be effectively utilized by everyone. Get as senior an executive sponsor as you can get to make the asks. Push for an explicit promise that these folks have time to give your pilot a fair shake and get a commitment to meet regularly. Book the actual check-in meetings all the

SLIGHTLY MORE EFFICIENT SELLING

way through the full time frame of the pilot so (1) they see you and the executive sponsor are aligned and (2) the meetings actually happen.

2. **Do NOT leave them alone**

    There's a spot of expectation-setting here because in the real implementation, there'll be full training, peer pressure, plus the knowledge that the company has invested and that they're doing this for real, not just make believe on top of their day job. So when designing your pilot, emphasize that you need more check-ins than they'd have in the real deal for the reasons above. That said… Check in LOADS. Every time you check in, test against the success criteria you agreed. Push hard against happy ears. Reward people for speaking out. Meet in smaller subgroups or no one will talk.

3. **Report your results in an easy-to-share format**

    Your pilot results are essentially a prototype of your business case. The intended recipient of this report is likely someone you haven't spoken to, but who holds the keys to your deal. Start with your one-page summary of the urgent important problem and how your Fix will work, then on page two talk about how the pilot proves your point. On the third page go straight into implementation of the main project so there's not a single second for them to ask themselves "what next?"

Quick Question: Should you charge for the pilot?

Maybe. You'll certainly drastically reduce the number of people who pilot. But for now let's assume you're not charging.

Multithreading

Getting to yes requires more than satisfying just one person; you need to prove your case to everyone on the buying committee. Most sellers know they should be multithreaded, but many don't really understand what it means.

Multithreaded does not just translate to your champion and their boss, and maybe the CFO at the end. You need to think up, down and across the buyer's power structure.

1. Who has the budget authority to pay for your solution?
2. Who is that person going to ask about your proposal?
3. Who will be responsible to implement and support (aka who has to do work)?

Once you have your list of roles, you need to put names to roles. This is where your champion performs one of their most important jobs.

In the previous chapter, we got to a point where your champion understands that DIY is riskier and less cost-effective than outsourcing the solution their problem to you. Part of that work was working out all the people who'd need to get their hands dirty.

Now you can remind your champion that you need to get these folks onboard with your nice low-effort Vendor approach.

"You know that outsourcing is the low-risk path, but these people need to know it too to make it happen. How should we get them to understand the UIP and the other DIHAP work we've done together?"

Make sure you explain why you'll need those other people and emphasize that this is to help the champion and you're not going to cut them out.

What if your champion doesn't want to make intros?

The first cause of gatekeeping is lack of trust. If your champion is unwilling to share who's who on their team, or unwilling to make intros to those folks, look first and confirm that they believe your analysis of their UIP and that they do actually want to buy your stuff.

Chances are you got ahead of yourself, and they're not ready yet to put their name on an introduction. Champions are a little bit like the mafia in this way. Any level of introduction is a tacit endorsement, and the guy on the inside is painfully aware that any bad faith from you later come directly back to them.

Other gatekeepers may be insecure about their position and want credit for the success you're about to bring their way. A good seller is already elevating these folks. Continue to show you're not going to cast them aside and you'll earn their trust.

You can even ask what they want out of this engagement and commit to incorporating their personal goals into your own objectives for the project.

The third kind of gatekeeper has no actual power. They were either told to keep you at arm's length from the power base, or they can't actually make the intro. Test this by showing them your implementation mutual action plan, highlighting the moments where you'll need those power figures to weigh in and ask how your champion is planning on getting them involved.

But most likely, it's the first thing. The decision makers don't actually really want your stuff, or they don't believe your analysis of their problem, and you got ahead of yourself.

You can reduce the risk of gatekeeping by establishing a core team for solving this problem as early as possible, made up of the key people from both the buyer team and your own team.

On your side is yourself as the rep, your implementation specialist and any technical scoping/ solutions engineer you might need. On their side is your champion (most likely the person actually impacted by the Urgent & Important Problem), the executive sponsor (the person at the buyer company with the budget or internal resources you need) and the implementation owner (Operations, IT, factory floor manager, whoever needs to do work to realize your fix).

With this team assembled, establish early on that you communicate with the whole group. A weekly email might be overkill, but regular status on progress towards the next milestone in your plan — if it's short and sweet — will keep their UIP and your fix top of mind, build your credibility as a capable partner, and make it much easier later on to get things done with the wider buying team.

Just sharing a MAP is perfect for this. Show what you're working towards, remind them what progress has been made and that you're on top of things. Always link back to your analysis of their problem (Root cause / Do Nothing / DIY / Vendor). This will also keep the monthly compounding cost of Do Nothing fresh in their minds.

Different messages for different roles

When you customize your POV for this specific deal, you should have a notion of how the different personas involved will benefit (or lose, or have to do work). You need those different flavors for your business case.

When you're multithreading, you need present a keyhole view of the UIP and your solution specific to the person you're talking to.

Ideally you're doing this hand-in-hand with your champion, so don't be afraid to tell them what you're doing. If they want your stuff, they should be happy to follow your lead.

 SLIGHTLY MORE EFFICIENT SELLING

There are two rules though

1. Don't be sneaky
2. Don't contradict yourself

There's nothing wrong with presenting different angles of a problem or a solution to meet the needs of the audience. Just make sure it's the same solution and you're not making different promises to different groups. Plan on them talking when you're not there or imagine they're all in the same room and you're asked to repeat what you said to one of them.

The trick here is to construct that POV so it's internally consistent, but at the same time, you can rotate it around so different people can see their own needs addressed. The way to do that is to position the UIP you're solving within the buyer's bigger initiatives. Always start your story with the bigger scope, then drill down to the detail level relevant to the person you're talking to.

No one sells alone

As a seller, you need relations with your buyers, but you also need to develop relations with the people from your own team. The good news is that these relationships can develop over multiple deals, but it does mean you need to be on your best behavior every deal.

Don't make the mistake of only working with one preferred Sales Engineer (SE). It may help your short term game to have a known dance partner, but your skills development stalls, and you'll be jacked when eventually that person moves on and you go from one partner to zero.

The Business Case

The best part of being Slightly More Efficient is that by the time you need a business case, it's 99% written, validated and socialized. If you have a customized POV, a clear analysis of the problem and an honest DIY assessment, then all you need is an inspiring photo for the cover, a one-page executive summary, and boom, you're done.

Your actual business case should be as short as possible. Figure that the people actually making the decision will read the Executive Summary at best, but they will ask their technical evaluators to read your whole analysis.

If you're really lucky, your champion will take all of the below and own the business case. It can happen. If you take a peek and it's got all the elements, then fantastic and you just need to present an order form.

But 90% of the time, this business case will be on your paper and it'll be on you to do the work.

Business Plan Table of Contents

- Exec Summary
- Problem Statement
- Fix Options
- Proof of Value
- Implementation Plan
- Money

The Executive Summary

This is your chance. Go heavy on the urgency and importance.

It's impossible to express your entire story on one page, so focus on what it takes for the reader to be able to say "if all this stuff is true, we should do it".

1. Lead with a headline they can remember, ideally including a meaningful number

2. Connect the dots from their stated priority to the urgent and important problem you and your champion identified as being the nexus of that priority

    "We heard from [role or name] that your priority is [priority]. Our thesis is [UIP+Fix]. We proved this out with [proof of value]. We compared costs of inaction vs. DIY vs. our approach and we predict [value] over [timeframe] and [cost of inaction] over the next [short term] if you maintain status quo. This document will prove out these points, and give a recommendation & key milestones of how to solve while minimizing risk and maximizing outcome over short, medium and long term.

3. Include a single chart that makes your case. Lead with numbers, not vague goodness.

4. Make a little box at the bottom to name-check all the buyer people you reviewed this with.

5. Be bold, be proud, be clear and include pricing (as a range for now). They're just gonna skip all the other pages and cut straight to the last page if you don't.

Problem Statement

Summarize your POV insights to explain the symptoms to root cause. Pull from your Do Nothing work for that specific buyer to show what will happen (and what has been happening) if they don't do something.

Fix Options

Lay out their options in a table. Compare and contrast DIY vs. Vendor for cost, benefit, timeline and change management requirements. At this point, your Vendor option really should be the incontrovertible best choice.

Proof of Value

Summarize the references, case studies (with links) or the pilot design & results.

Implementation Plan

This section will make you stand out head and shoulders above the competition. Including an Implementation plan shows you think ahead, which is a very attractive trait in a potential business parter. It takes risk and uncertainty out of the equation, which is the main thing the CFO is looking for, and if you do it right, it sets you up for a faster time to value — and thus a faster time to expansion. All good things.

Money

This gets a little more sophisticated. Read on.

Money — the price of value and the cost of risk

As an astute seller with a quota, you've probably noticed we haven't talked about money yet. Now's the time.

We'll figure out the price based on the value you're providing over some specific time frames, and discuss how to discount based on the buyer's perceived risk.

Value based pricing

In the business case, you need to put down an actual price, or least a range of pricing. But you should do it in context of the value you're providing and you should show your work.

The good news is during the Do Nothing and DIY evaluations you already established this value. So now the question is how much would your customer pay for that value and how much of a discount will they demand to cover the cost of their risk in case everything you said was wrong?

1. What's the cost of inaction over short and long term?
2. How long will it take to see value?
3. What is the chance that everything you said comes true?

What most value-sellers miss is that the value of your fix is not the anchor that you think it is.

Your actual price ceiling is the buyer's DIY cost (or competitors, but we'll cover that in a moment). That's why you have to show DIY cost in your business case. They'll get the value whether they go in-house or outsource. What you're competing against is the cost of that DIY.

It's not just dollars though — if it were, vendors would lose a lot more deals. You get to include the total cost of ownership, including development, implementation and upkeep. Then the job of your business case is to prove that it's less risky - and ultimately less expensive — to go with you versus DIY (and competing vendors) .

It's really important to include timeframes in your value calculations. You need to be convincing based on the short term on its own, and let the long term be the gravy. This is because most businesses don't think seriously about anything more than two quarters ahead, because no one really knows what the future looks like, so the further out you go, the further your risk factor moves up an exponential curve.

So include two time frames: 1 to 2 quarters and 12-18 months, with the timer starting at Go Live. You should only be going further out if you're working on an eight figure deal.

The above also includes relative impact of your solution to the buyer's daily life. How many zeros do you need to be offering to get their attention?

Both your problem and your value need to be worth their time. You did the work on the problem side when determining this was an important problem. You need to do one final check in the value pricing stage too because if your solution is so expensive it's only saving them $1000 a year, they're not going to do it.

That significance line is going to be entirely determined by the dollar values your economic decision maker deals with in their daily job.

Discounting for buyer risk

Everyone claims to have amazing ROI, but buyers know not every ROI number can be trusted. So your price has to include a discount for risk. You'll hear the phrase "even if only 10% of what I showed comes true…" That's the risk discount. There is risk around the magnitude of the cost of the problem, the success rate of the proposed solution to recapture all that lost money and the dollar cost of change management in effort, lost productivity during implementation and opportunity cost.

In your spreadsheet this risk factor will manifest as the margin between the value of the fix and the price you're charging.

Department operating budget	$100M
Cost of problem	$10M
Solution price	$2M
Cost of change management	$0.5M
Nominal margin for value to be recaptured	$7.5M

It's up to the buyer to decide how much they want to discount for risk. It's 100% on the customer because it's literally and solely the percentage of how much they believe you.

• If they believe you 100%	That's $7.5.M of value, or 7.5% of their operating budget. Easy. Let's do it!
• If they believe you 50%	You're offering $2.5M of value; only 2.5% of their total operating budget. Much harder decision.
• If they only believe you 25%	You're only offering $0.5M above a $2M cost. Much safer to stick with Do Nothing or DIY.

Here's how I explain risk factor to a customer

> *If I had a machine where you put a $5 bill in one end and a $20 bill came out the other side, everyone would find budget and buy it.*
>
> *Any hesitation in buying my thing is that no matter how good my proof is, you don't 100% believe my numbers. That's understandable: every vendor promises the same $5-in-$20-out. So when you look at my pricing, even building in some pretty aggressive disbelief, what do the numbers say? If you only believe 50%, does it still make sense given the known cost of doing nothing? 75%? That number is your risk factor.*

Make sure you include a risk factor for all three options of Do Nothing, DIY and Vendor so you'll have a closer apples-to-apple-to-apples comparison.

Discount Levers

The business case should also have your discount levers printed on the page.

- **Quantity** — you'll reduce unit price if they buy more
- **Duration** — you'll reduce price if they commit to a longer term
- **Faster** — you'll reduce the price if they sign on your timeline instead of theirs.

Side note: I hate reducing price for a faster signature. It fundamentally shifts your conversation from being buyer-centric to seller-centric. But the fact is you need to make your number and you're willing to pay for that quota assurance.

Final thoughts on the Business Case

You can't price based on your costs

We've talked a lot about two-way streets in this book, and most of them help you as a seller. But there is a cost of selling on value. In value selling, you're purposefully not talking about what it costs to make the product, you're only talking about the impact. That's the right thing to focus on, but you have to be aware that it means your claims of "my costs are going up so I have to charge more" have zero impact on your customer's perceived value from your product.

Instead, focus on decreasing their Risk Factor. It's the easiest input to change in their price value equation. Now your cost of goods sold should be below the noise floor of your pricing strategy. If it isn't, and your value-add is so thin that an increase in costs forces an increase in price then you need to find a new product to sell.

Take heart — if your costs are increasing, then chances are the value you're imparting is also increasing, since the macro impacting you is probably also exacerbating your customer's urgent and important problem (which is good for you as the fixer of that problem).

Format

This is your document. You might co-create the DIHAP and the Proof of Value under your champion's name (and you'll borrow from and even quote those folks extensively), but at some point you need to say "this is us and this is what we stand for"

Saying that, you should ask your champion if the buyer's company culture leans towards slide decks or Word-style documents and format your analysis to suit. Whichever way you go, make sure you have easy links to the supporting materials — the mutual action plan, case studies, POC detail etc.

Time Matters

I said you need to include two time frames in your value calculations.

That first time frame is important for you too because it's your opportunity to build in an expectation of expansion early. In your mutual action plan, include a check point for that first time to value. During pre-sales, this shows you're confident in your dates and your time to value. This is reassuring to your buyer.

Then when that checkpoint date arrives, you'll do two things

1. **Ask for a referral** — This is "thank God I gave you money day". You kept your word, fixed the problem. You've proven that the buyer was smart to trust you. They'll want to show gratitude, so let them know a referral is the best way to show their appreciation.

2. **Look for the expansion** — You proved you can be trusted, you showed you do indeed sell $5-in-$20-out money printing machines, so your next proposal inherits that performance, which comes with much lower risk, which makes it much easier to find budget. Who wouldn't want a second money printing machine if it's been proven they work?

One thing — between kickoff and TGIGYMD, you need to make sure that your CS colleagues deliver on that early value marker. Your expansion and referral depend on it.

This is yet another reason why internal seller-side multithreading is so important. And a great example of why capitalism works so well. Your profit motive turns you into a source of pressure for your CS colleagues to deliver instead of just hoping they perform for the self-satisfaction of a job well done. The invisible hand extant.

We'll talk more about this in a couple of chapters.

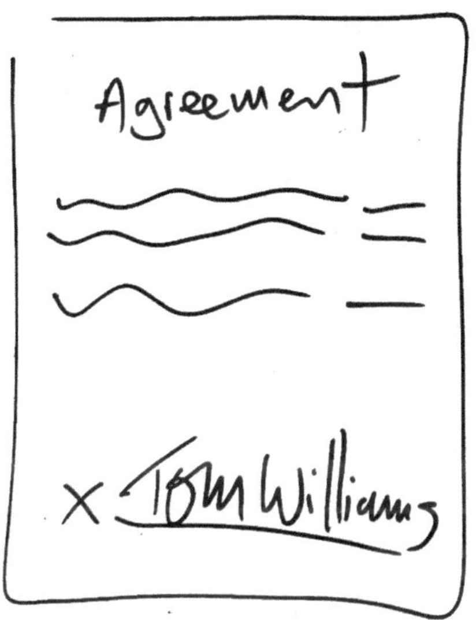

CHAPTER 6 | Signed!

What can go wrong?

Value is agreed, price is fine, implementation details are all put to bed. What can go wrong?

SO. MANY. THINGS.

It's important to remember that at this point, we've moved on from the buyer wanting the thing to actually making it happen. The benefits of your fix are no longer on trial. This is purely buying mechanics. Speed is the key here — along with making sure everyone is on the same page the whole time.

So what does it take to not blow it?

Even if paper process doesn't kill your deal, there's a huge risk that it slows you down enough so that you miss either your timeline (ie: missing your end of quarter) or worse, you miss the buyer's timeline and they don't need your approach anymore.

The first thing to remember is the buyer has never bought from you. But they have bought other stuff. There may not be an official process, but they have bought in the past. So they know *something* about what it will take.

At the same time, you've sold your thing a hundred times, just not to these people. So you also know something about what it will take.

So while during all these conversations over the past weeks and months, you've been trying to build up a picture of all the mechanics your buyer needs to walk through to buy your stuff, it's still probably only half right — and even less if you're working with less experienced buyers.

Check your MAP - Who can say no on the buyer's team?

You've been halfheartedly sharing the mutual action plan (MAP) all these weeks, but at this point you've got to get serious and get detailed, otherwise you're going to miss something that delays or kills your deal. The longer you procrastinate on this, more you'll increase the risk that paper process gums up your deal.

Let's take a look at the biggest deal killers you're likely to bump up against:

• IT / Infosec
• Implementation
• Legal
• Procurement

IT/ Infosec

Like buying IBM, hardly anyone gets fired for saying "NO". It's less work, less risk, less blame, less stress.

Detractors can hard-no a project in one second with next to no accountability just by saying "security". This is why good sellers bring the buyer's IT team into the deal real early. That and the fact that if you leave them out of the loop, they're going think you're trying to do an end run around them. Then they get resentful and predisposed to say no.

So when you're talking with the buyer's IT team, make sure you are never asking for a yes or no on your solution. Instead, make sure they're making a choice between two options.

- **DIY** — which involves a ton of work and creates a thousand new risk vectors
- **Your approach** — less work and less risk

(The option of Do Nothing is already out because you showed the cost was too high to bear)

Buyer's implementation team

This is the team you need to get your solution live internally. Maybe enablement, maybe IT, maybe Ops. The problem is they already have projects. You don't want to be blindsided by the customer's implementation team saying "oh, actually we can't do this for 6 months." If you check in regularly and have a clear path to success, you'll minimize their anxiety about taking on the work.

Confirm, reconfirm then reconfirm again. And keep reminding them your approach is less work than DIY.

Legal

I don't know much about legal except that I'm extremely skeptical, especially when more junior counsel are involved. Legal's job is supposed to be risk mitigation, but sometimes it almost seems like they're afraid that if they don't find something to pick at, their leaders will assume they're not working hard enough.

The upshot is that it's rare to find a contract that isn't marked up in some way.

All that red can cause heart palpitations, especially if you're up against a deadline to close the deal. But if you think of that red ink as stemming from a junior lawyer just trying to show they're contributing something to the conversation, then it's less dramatic.

As a seller you'll start to see the same redlines in every deal. Treat them like any other objection. Or maybe compile them as a sales team and go to your legal and say "this requirement is slowing down all our deals".

One thing I've seen is that junior counsel will list every single thing that could possibly possibly be a problem, whereas more senior counsel will apply reasonable judgement and let the unlikely stuff slide.

As a seller staring at a sea of red markup coming back from your buyer, there's no harm in asking your champion where they think this is coming from.

"Lot of red here. It's putting your Fix at risk. There's nothing actually controversial in this contract; is it possible that legal put a junior person on this? Is there anyone you can gut check with?"

Note how this brings in your buyer to help. They're going to have 100x more success solving this than you.

Procurement

Procurement is already mad at you. From their perspective some amateur from within their company came and told them to buy something that they hadn't planned on buying. If the company really needed it, procurement would have already procured it goddammit.

Add to this that I'm pretty sure that junior procurement people get paid based on how many tears of frustration they can extract from vendors.

They are definitely compensated on overall discount negotiated.

It's so dumb, and it's the only reason I would ever say unrequited discount is ever justified. Because of course, if you hear that your buyer has a procurement team that you're going to have to deal with, all you're going to do is mark up your price by 20% so they get their 20% discount.

So dumb.

It's even worse with outsourced procurement.

Again, the answer is to send in your executive sponsor to fight the battle.

One point here — procurement shouldn't be a surprise. When you're working on the DIY vs. Vendor analysis, ask about procurement. Work from the assumption that you're working with your champion against a common enemy whose knee-jerk "no" is putting their fix at risk.

Internal people will have much more sway than you will (considering you will have zero sway), so when you're setting out the roles for each person in your core buying team, include internal procurement liaison and copy those guys on every bit of crazy that Procurement tries to throw at you.

Who else can wreck your deal? Your own team

It is absolutely possible for your own team to scuttle a deal.

The easiest way is if you or one of your colleagues made a promise that the org can't keep.

Here are a few of the scenarios where you might say "yes" to close the deal, but that you will almost certainly regret before the end of the deal.

- **Free Professional Services**
  You know PS gets discounted to hell anyway, and you need a sweetener. So you offer free PS. But PS has their own cost to serve that they need to mind. The problem is you get what you pay for, so you'll end up with a poorly-serviced customer who never sees the value you promised. You will be blamed, you'll have to spend personal capital to get it fixed and you'll get no referrals.

- **Implementation Timeline**
  Customer says they need the fix implemented by a certain date. You say no problem. Deal Desk checks with Implementation team, and discover they're already committed to other projects. The deal can fall through at the last minute, or you have angry implementation team, and again, resentful customers looking to you for answers.

- **Escape Clause**
  Some buyers want the ability to cancel early if you don't meet your benchmarks. Totally reasonable, but it sticks CS with a massive responsibility. This one would get caught in legal when the buyer adds it last minute, referring to a verbal conversation you barely remember, but remember well enough to be unable to deny.

For each of these, the solution is clean and simple: collaborate early. Make sure your core deal team is aware of any side conversations you've initiated with various folks from the buyer side so there are no self-inflicted wounds.

Competitive Hail Marys & buyers' remorse

If you found out a deal you'd worked on for months was going to go to one of your competitors, but that they were stuck in legal, would you say "well fought sir, the better seller won" and let your competitor have the business, or would you throw some super-FUD into the mix to try and open up the decision?

Your competitor feels the same about your soon-to-be-signed-but-not-actually-signed deal. They'll be throwing everything they have, not to win the deal, but to wreck your deal so they can get back in there.

Just another reason why you need to move as fast as possible through paper process.

Add to this sea of chaos the strong possibility that your buyer may feel the beginnings of buyer's remorse. The paper process window is the first time that you have to start keeping the promises you made.

"Easier and less risky than doing it yourself" was your mantra. How will they feel if Infosec, Legal, Implementation, and Procurement all start kicking up?

What's insidious is you can't keep going back to your business case. You already made the case and they already signed off. If you keep going on about it, they might think you doubt the work.

This is all about execution. Over-communicate.

Any problem, you be the one to find it and fix it.

Keep on your team like a hawk to stay true to commitments.

Use your MAP to reassure your buyer during longer stretches of apparent inaction (looking at you Legal!) that you are, in fact, exactly on track.

A weekly email is all you need. Include a screen shot of the MAP with a "you are here" even if nothing has changed from last week. You're communicating that you're on track and that you're steering the ship.

Keep close to your champion and listen for seeds of doubt or poison pills coming from other members of the buying team, especially if there was anyone who had endorsed either DIY or a competitor. Bring those folks into the core team so they can see you're addressing their concerns and moving forward, creating more distance every week that a competitor would have to catch up with.

No deal is done until it's done.

Final note here. It's so tempting to breathe easy when a senior exec from the buying team wants your thing. But executives don't always think every purchase through carefully. They definitely don't run each detail down to its logical conclusion.

So your executive sponsor can easily say "I want it" but Legal or IT coming up with a single blocker in the buying process can derail the deal enough for your sponsor to withdraw their support for fear of getting caught up in a tangle of internal politics.

Coach your champion to stay involved to make it more likely that any Legal and IT naysayers are coming to your champion about their objections instead of going straight to Power; then ask / beg / bribe your champion to not brush their concerns under the carpet, but to tell you so you can work together on a solution.

Coach that champion to let you and them give that weekly update to the senior Power. Walk the line between communication and maintaining momentum.

Final final final — just deliver what you promised.

Deliver it on time and stay on budget.

———

CHAPTER 7 | Smooth Handovers

It's not your job, but it is your problem

The handover window is so risky. Not only has the buyer given you their money, they've also put their personal reputation — maybe even their career — into your hands.

So the buyer is on edge, maybe feeling buyer remorse, second-guessing their decision and hoping they bet right when they chose you. Meanwhile, you feel the opposite. You closed a deal, made some money, got that much closer to quota. You won! Net net? There's no time when you're further apart from the buyer than handover.

And that's dangerous.

The problem is after the deal closes, everyone's interests have diverged again.

It's tempting to say your job is done here, and just throw the deal over the wall for your colleagues in post-sales to handle, but doing that is a huge mistake, both for the customer and for yourself.

Ensuring a smooth handover will cement your reputation as a long term provider of value.

It also makes life easier for your colleagues, which never goes amiss in an organization. Finally, and most importantly, a smooth handover boosts the chances of success for your buyer almost infinitely. That's going to make them happy, which then makes referrals, renewals and expansions easier.

Post-sales team needs vs. buyer needs

Your number one job as seller is to facilitate. In pre-sale, that was just facilitating the buyer's evaluation team, and maybe a sales engineer from your side. Here in post-sale you need to accommodate the needs of your own implementation and customer success teams... when it's not even your deal anymore.

So where do you stand right after the ink dries? Your buyer wants to get all the things you promised. So they expect ultimate white-glove-treatment super fast.

The implementation team is measured on cost-to-serve and closed tickets. So they want to get in and out as fast as possible and onto the next work order. This disconnect has the potential for disaster unless you can realign the two sides with a little transparency and expectation setting.

1

Set clear expectations

Way early in the sales process, talk about implementation. This will help you set expectations with both your customer and your team for what customer success and implementation can and can't do, and puts time frames around what will happen. That means less friction during implementation.

Side benefit: it will also reduce customer anxiety during pre-sale, because going deep on implementation shows you're not just there to sell, you're with them for the whole ride.

2

Make handover super easy for your post-sales team

During pre-sales you had a high-level view of timeframe and the milestones you need to hit to fix the problem. Ideally you did that in a MAP, and ideally that MAP had some milestones after Close. If that's the case, your handover is literally written down already.

Armed with that MAP, invest time in a good handover to your colleagues.

- ☐ Use the DIHAP worksheet you created with the buyer to guide the handover.
- ☐ Summarize the customer's priorities and what's at stake for them.
- ☐ Share call recordings or documents where you really got to the heart of what the customer is looking for.
- ☐ Cover how they'd have fixed the problem themselves so PS knows how technical the other team is.
- ☐ Share any proof-of-value work you did to show how the customer thinks and the level of polish they're expecting.
- ☐ Share any specific language or acronyms you picked up so PS doesn't have to ask dumb questions that hurt their credibility and slow down implementation.
- ☐ Be honest about the people. If there's a jerk, don't let your colleagues just waltz in unawares. This might be the one place where you don't write everything down.

3 Intro the teams early

Early on during Education when the buyers are still evaluating the merits of your approach vs. DIY and leaning towards you, you should bring in an Implementation leader and a Customer Success leader. If your org does Account Managers (aka Farmers vs. AE Hunters) then bring in an AM first line manager too.

Emphasize that these leaders won't be the folks actually handling the account, but that they're the people that ultimately take responsibility for the successful realization of value. This is key. Along with yourself, these are the accountable people.

This does three things.

- First, it demonstrates you're serious as a coordinated single organization, with an army behind you ready to deliver the promises you make.

- Second, your senior post-sales people make a better impression than the more junior person likely to be put on the account. At the same time, meeting the customer will make it easier for your senior post-sales people to assign the right people to the account.

- Third, the actual account team will be held to a higher standard. Just knowing that the customer has been intro'd to their manager, and has an open invitation to call, means they'll take the extra effort to execute.

- Sneaky 4th benefit — you look good here too. Those senior leaders will remember you as a thorough executive who reduces risk and delivers customers with reasonable expectations and no surprises.

And all because you organized a 30 minute meeting 5 months ago.

Trust but verify

You could facilitate the easiest handover in the world, and your post-sale colleagues could still blow the relationship. You need insurance.

You need to stay in the loop. Remember those weekly emails you were sending to the Collaboration Core Team showing successful progress-to-plan on your MAP? Insist that the Professional Services (PS) / Customer Success (CS) team continue that email to the same group, cc'ing you.

You should be right there from Kickoff to Go Live, all the way through first value demonstrating your high "say / do" ratio.

Make sure CS and PS don't try to bury you and the Collaboration Core Team in paperwork. Set the expectation that you and the Collaboration Core team need enough detail to know the company is honoring the promises you made.

This is a 10 min per week effort. You're not doing anything more than making sure your buyer knows you're still engaged and making sure your PS colleagues know you're holding them accountable to the timelines and quality that you promised.

You might have private check-ins with your Champion to get a backchannel on how implementation is going, then you can report any concerns to the lead of the implementation. Or that lead's boss if you need to escalate.

Hello folks, this is your captain speaking

When you're on a commercial flight, there is a 100% certainty that the captain is going to get on the intercom. Captains do this because they need you to know a couple things

1. You're in good hands
2. This flight is going to land safe and sound

As a passenger, I want to hear that reassurance. I also want to know if it's going to be a little bumpy as we cross the mountains, when to look out the window to see something interesting, whether we're going to arrive on time, and whether or not I can expect the cabin lights to be turned off.

What I DON'T want as a passenger is the full flight prep checklist. That list has a whole lot of things that can go wrong with this metal tube rocketing through the upper atmosphere.

Personally I don't like it when the captain explains that we're sitting on the runway because some engine part fell off, and they're gonna go find a new one and stick it back on real quick.

I mention this because the executives who made the decision to buy your stuff don't really want the nitty gritty dirty details of implementation. They want to know when to look out the left side of the plane to see the natural wonder passing by beneath and they want to know in advance if there's any turbulence expected so they don't spill their drink.

In short, when you're laying out your implementation plan, stick to the higher level actions on both the buyer and seller side. Be honest about effort and timelines, but don't drown in detail.

Then outline your executive go-live communications accordingly and before you know it, smooth handover is accomplished and you can get to referrals and expansion.

TGIGYM!

CHAPTER 8 | Thank God I Gave You Money!

From Go Live to First Value to Expansion

The deal is done! The customer is handed off. You deserve some time off.

And….OK. I hope you enjoyed your break.

Even though the customer is now implemented, they still haven't seen that first value you promised, so as a good partner, you're still on the hook. But there's stuff in it for you too.

You need to get to your buyer to Thank God I Gave You Money Day.

The key here is to bring your AM & CS colleagues on the journey with you. You may have handed over the customer, but the customer hasn't handed over you. You're the one they trust, who they shared their pains and tribulations with. The post-sales team just hasn't banked the time that you have.

But don't worry.

Just as you weren't responsible for the actual implementation, you're not responsible for actually getting the customer to value; but you do need to keep tabs and ring the alarm if something is going wrong. Rather than being a threat, your post-sales peers should relish this. As the person who's worked with the buyers the longest, you're more likely than the AM or the CS lead to get honest feedback. Act as the back channel and give the real story to your post-sale colleagues. As the buyer sees that their contacts in post-sale are as intellectually honest and capable as you are — and ideally actually more knowledgeable about what they need in post-sale life — you'll see a natural move over from you to them.

You do need to make sure you don't take on post-sales work. If your buyer asks you to run an enablement session, CS would be thrilled to let you do the work. You might even do a better job because you know the personalities. Resist! Rip off that band-aid. Hand that hot potato over to CS and be transparent with your buyer about who does what and why it's important that they get to know their CS manager.

Countdown to TGIGYMD

As a rep you've guided this process from inkling of a problem to deeper analysis of root cause to evaluation of best way to fix to handover to implementation. But you've always had your eye laser focused on that first value realization, aka Thank God I Gave you Money Day.

So did it work? Did your buyer get the value you promised? Are they thanking God they gave you money?

Only the buying team gets to decide, but you still have influence.

At handover, there's a natural tendency for engagement to drop off. Your senior buyers made the decision, and now they're off to the next urgent & important problem. So just as you handed over the day-to-day to your AM or CS counterpart, so on the buyer side the senior decision makers hand over to a junior administrator.

This is a huge risk and missed opportunity for you. It's vitally important that you get a commitment from the buyer core team (champion, exec sponsor and head implementer) to stay engaged all the way through TGIGYMD.

They're probably not going to give you the time for a standing meeting, but you should be able to secure a check in for three key milestones.

1. **Go live** — report how implementation went and reaffirm the success metrics, especially if you learned anything during implementation.
2. **Mid-way to first value** — are the metrics trending the right direction to show you're fixing the urgent and important problem? Is any course correction recommended?
3. **First value date** — Achieved? Champagne all around…. Or some great reasons why a course correction is needed, and detail on what that course is.

If the Account Manager wants to own this meeting, that's fine, but you need to be there. In between these buyer core team check-ins, hold your post-sales colleagues accountable to deliver what you promised. And if there's a problem, make sure you're the one making noise, not the customer.

It's only on that glorious day when the problem is fixed and the value is delivered that your buyer will finally breathe a sigh of relief that they made the right choice trusting you.

Now you can ask for some stuff.

Referral

We already said way back at the start of the book that referrals are the best lead source. But if you're systematic, they might be the only source you need. Let's set up the big picture first, then look at how to make the individual referral ask.

Macro Step One: Goals & metrics

The only way to get better at something is practice and metrics. So let's create some metrics to measure so you can hone your referral game. Keep track of these metrics over time and compete with your colleagues.

- **Ask Ratio**
  What percent of deals did you ask for a referral? Some customers are jerks, some deals just didn't go smoothly. This number represents your at-bats, so higher is better. There's no reason this shouldn't be 90% of all your closed-won deals, but at the beginning surely 50% of deals went well enough and you built up enough rapport to make some level of ask.

SLIGHTLY MORE EFFICIENT SELLING

- **Success Rate**

  For all the referral asks you made, how many opportunities did you create?

- **Lead Source Ratio**

  Where else are your leads coming from? This is just a gee-up to keep up the pressure. Cold leads are going to be 1000x harder to win than a warm referral, so tracking how much time you're wasting on the hard road might remind you to put more effort into the easy ones.

- **Referrer Profile**

  You probably won't track this as diligently, but understanding the type of person — be that a job role or a personality — will help you know who to spend your effort on. Not just at the window of the referral, but earlier too. Think about that. Your best referrer type might not be your champion, but might be someone who jumps jobs a lot - like a fellow seller or a technocrat who doesn't worry so much about giving away competitive advantage. Now you'll know who to invest more time with during the next sales cycle.

The Ask itself

You can only ask for a referral after you quantifiably and definitively delivered on Thank God I Gave You Money Day. Everyone on the buyer team is breathing sighs of relief that they trusted you, their problem is fixed or well on its way to fixed, even the detractors are begrudgingly acknowledging that you were right and they were wrong.

This can't be just "Hey, who should I talk to?" That's better than nothing, but it's not slightly more efficient because not only are you asking for a favor, you're asking your referrer to do work for which they get no benefit.

Do your homework, and right after TGIGYMD, make your ask:

> *"I've been working on my POV on these three companies [A,B and C]. You know some of those folks don't you? Do you have anything to add about [their urgent and important problem]? Is there anyone at any of those companies you could intro me to? I think you might know Paul?"*

A couple of assumptions pre-baked into this:

1. Select companies from your book of business that your referrer is likely to know and or share commonalities with their role or industry, but obviously don't name check any direct competitors.

2. Check LinkedIn to see who your referrer knows so you can suggest specific people.

3. Don't limit your ask to one person per company. At least ask your Champion and the technical implementor. Try your best to establish a good enough relationship with the buyer executive sponsor. Your A,B & C might be different companies or different people depending on the profile of the referrer you're talking to. I might be more targeted with just my A's and B's if I'm talking with a buyer super high up the executive power structure.

Expansion

Remember back when you were still establishing trust with your buyers, you read up on minimizing risk and probably said "let's start small and low risk"?

Remember you added a date to expand in that MAP, otherwise you just succeeded in selling a cut rate version of your product?

That time is now. Not next year.

As soon as you hit TGIGYMD, remind your Core team that this was just the proof of your root cause knowledge and that the big value, the real value, awaits. Show them you nailed everything you promised, and start the next exploration of DIY or Outsource.

If your team is strictly Hunter / Farmer, then be happy in the knowledge that you paid it forward and set up your AM colleague for an easy win. If you're a little more aggressive, tell your manager that you want to keep the account through TGIGYMD, arguing that you'll be able to deliver the expansion faster than a new Account Manager who hasn't had the time yet to build up trust.

After all, the deal doesn't end til the customer gets value.

Deal retrospective

It might be tempting to think Handover is your retrospective, and it's true you can pull a lot of the facts from your handover into your Retro. But yo! — the deal doesn't end at close. And you can't retro something that isn't finished. The retro needs to include all the following:

1. **Summary**
   1 page summary of all the below. Should be easy.

2. **Insights for POV**
   Did you learn anything that should be incorporated into your POV template?

3. **Insights for MAP**
   Did the MAP change much during the deal? Did you change any milestones or did something take longer? Could you update the MAP template to stop that happening next time? Don't just add things here. Maybe taking something away is the right answer.

4. **Insights for Value**
   What value metrics did the customer actually attain? Should you edit any value calc inputs?

5. **Insights for Seller Team**
   Did your colleagues deliver? Did anyone drop the ball or exceed expectations?

6. **Insights for Referral**
   Who said yes, and was it a quality lead? Maybe update your Referral Profile.

7. **Reference: Do Nothing / DIY/ Vendor Spreadsheet & Business Case**
   Already created. Zero work.

These Retrospectives are your personal IP. Keep them close, learn from them. Teach from them. Write a book. Send me half the money.

TL;DR

Hi Sellers!!

You made it through 111 pages of me talking about how to sell stuff. I'm honored.

I'll recap the whole thing in case you're actually from the buyer side and just skipped to the last page to see if there's a good bit.

Before you talk to a single buyer, you need to create a point of view about the industry you serve and the problems you fix. You need to be able to explain the root causes of problems and how to fix them in a way that doesn't include your product.

Then find a company with an urgent and important problem that you think you can fix. Show them the root cause of their problem to build trust and work with them to compare risk, effort and cost of Do Nothing, DIY or buying your solution.

Build a business case for your approach vs. DIY.

Coordinate the entire buying team and selling team towards that moment after contract and go-live when the customer sees their first value — Thank God I Gave You Money Day. Invest in a smooth handover, but stay involved until TGIGYMD.

Then, and only then, run a retrospective over the whole deal, update your templates based on what you learned and mindfully ask for a referral.

Take a breath, be proud you made the world slightly more efficient, then start over.

Switch Sides

Sellers: *Go understand how buyers learn about their problems and think about how you could make their journey slightly more efficient*

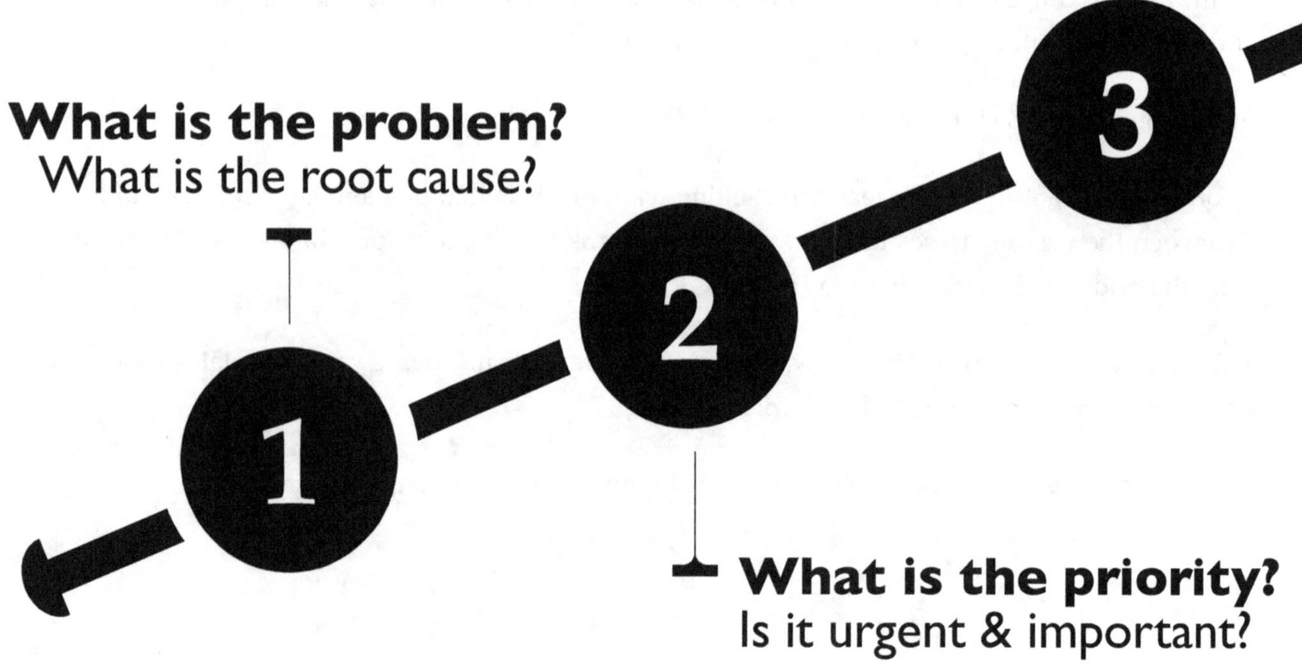

HOW THIS BOOK WORKS

Buying and selling are two sides of the same coin: to understand one, you need to understand the other. This flip book works the same way. Read this side first, then flip the book upside down to see the world from the opposite perspective. Good news: they meet in the middle.

WHO IS THIS BOOK FOR

The ideas in this book really only apply to people buying and selling fairly expensive stuff. That means you're solving problems in mid-to-large size companies with typical deal values of at least $50,000. The insights apply to any industry, not just venture-funded software companies. That said, a lot of the innovation around buyer-seller collaboration comes from SaaS, so apologies in advance if any tech jargon slipped through.

ABOUT TOM

After 23 years of sales & marketing inside startups, enterprise software, electronics manufacturing and marketing agencies, Tom is focused on making the global economy slightly more efficient by improving how we buy and sell.

Tom was co-founder of DealPoint, the first sales collaboration solution for customer-centric sales teams. He sold to Clari, the folks who created the revenue operations category and who now make the best revenue platform in the industry.

Tom talks, listens, parents and squashes in Portland, Oregon and Brighton, England.

SLIGHTLY MORE EFFICIENT

BUYING

A practical guide to working with vendors to make rational,
low-risk, cost-effective and defendable buying decisions

Tom Williams

SLIGHTLY MORE EFFICIENT

Slightly More Efficient Selling | Slightly More Efficient Buying
How Sellers and Buyers Should Collaborate to Fix Urgent & Important Problems

Published 2024
ISBN: 979-8-218-53386-1

Savvy Reckless Publishing
Portland, Oregon, USA

No valid complaint since 2016

SLIGHTLY MORE EFFICIENT

Common Foreword

Buying and selling are two sides of the same coin, so why are there so few books about buying? And how could you even write about one without referencing the other?

I don't know, so this book has two front covers. Flip it to read about the opposite perspective. Good news: they meet in the middle.

At the end of the day, if someone learns they have a problem, then they have exactly three options: they can do nothing, they can fix it themselves, or they find a partner to help them.

Buyers are people who find themselves needing to make this decision. Sellers are people whose job is to help buyers evaluate those options, admittedly with a strong bias towards option C.

My goal with this book is to make that process slightly more efficient. I believe we'll do this by being more open with each other about how best to work together. I also believe if we get it right, then we can literally boost the global economy and bump human productivity by a couple points. No pressure!

You can read this book as either a buyer or a seller, but ideally, you'll read both sides to understand how your counterparty thinks. My only ask is that you use this knowledge for good. Don't go ripping off the other side just because I told you what they're thinking.

Tom Williams, Portland, August 2024

CONTENTS — BUYING SIDE

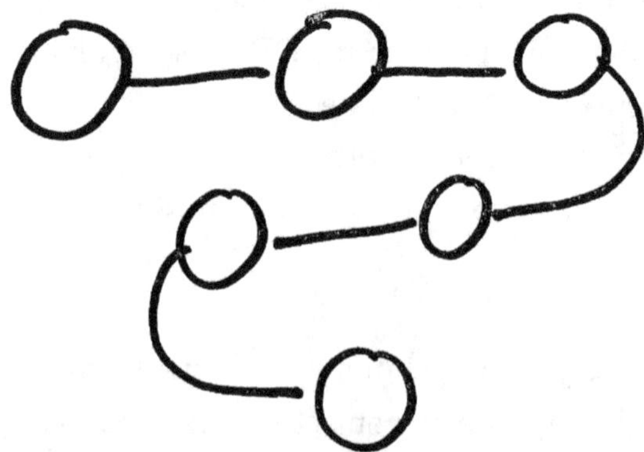

INTRODUCTION | Buying is Hard

It's definitely harder than selling

Amazon has over 5000 books about selling. Powell's Books here in Portland has a whole room on the topic. There's any number of selling gurus, consultants and courses to take.

But buying is actually the harder job.

You have all the risk. You're the one who's going to have to go to battle to get budget, and you're the one who's going to have to drive change, not just for the first month, but forevermore vigilant against your colleagues backsliding to their old ways. If it goes bad, the fallout is on you, not the guy who sold you the wrong thing.

So why so few books about how to buy stuff?

In this book, I want to share what I know about 6 things

1. The sketchy tricks that Sellers will try to pull on you
2. How to evaluate if you have a problem more objectively
3. How to evaluate your options to fix: Do nothing, DIY, or go with a vendor
4. How to drive internal consensus and get to a decision
5. How to develop a real change management plan
6. How to evaluate how it all went so you have notes for next time

By revealing the low road of sneaky sales techniques, I'll remove their effectiveness, which will force reps to move up to the high road of being an actually helpful in fixing problems.

By helping you understand how to evaluate problems down to the root cause, you'll be better equipped to fix those problems. Whether you start the hunt for a solution to a problem yourself or you got hooked by a seller who's trying to convince you to buy their stuff, having a rubric to evaluate your problem and the potential solutions to address it will make your decision slightly less emotional, and ultimately make it far more likely that you actually fix the problem and make your life better.

By getting better around collaboration from bottom to top, left to right all across your org you'll be more successful in making that fix actually happen. You're competing against other initiatives, other personalities and probably other politics that have nothing to do with this problem you're trying to fix. But if you're smart, you can navigate these waters with ease and get what you're asking for.

Finally, I really want to emphasize that deciding on the fix is the start of the actual journey, not the end. Change management is the bane of every fix, so let's figure out how to make that smoother.

Whether you're doing it yourself or outsourcing the solution to a vendor, you probably haven't implemented the thing before, so you're likely to either over- or under- estimate the effort.

Understanding the effort of making a change will help you weigh your options more realistically, and is guaranteed to leave you in a better position than if you act without thinking about how it's going to rollout.

By the way, there's an arc here — you will overestimate the effort during those stages when you don't really want the thing, and you'll underestimate when you do want it. Blame human nature, but getting it wrong in either direction does yourself and your colleagues a disservice, so let's do what we can to get it right.

Buying Journey Theory

Before we get into how to make decisions, I want to share an overview of what sellers are taught about buyers. This should help you understand your own buying process, plus give you some insider info on what your sales counterpart is thinking.

Every buying decision goes through seven stages. In the sales world, they call this the *buying journey*. Every stage is a Go/ No Go, with a couple of the stages branching in different directions depending on decisions such as "Do I choose DIY or bring in vendors".

Of course, each stage can have multiple sub-stages with different stakeholders putting their oar in. And it's really important to remember that while time only flows in one direction, the buying journey is anything but linear. Decisions made can be unmade just as quickly as new people or new information come to light.

The easiest way to follow along is to think about something you bought recently and map what you did back to these steps.

1

AWARENESS ➼ I (may) have a problem

This is the first inkling that something is wrong, or at least, something could be better. But there are a lot of problems in the world. You need to learn more before you make any decisions. You might have come to this awareness of a problem on your own, or someone else might make you aware. It doesn't really matter. What does matter is that you're now aware of a problem (or at least a potential problem) and you've accepted responsibility to learn more and see if some action is needed.

2

EDUCATION ➼ This is a real problem, and it's both urgent & important

Time to do some research. You need to understand the problem better to figure out what level of time & resources you should put into fixing it. Essentially you're taking your rough notes from the Awareness stage and expanding them into a quantified UIP - Urgent & Important Problem. Educate yourself on the root cause(s) of the problem and what the better future looks like. Ideally you can quantify that desired future with a dollar value per year to help you understand the severity of your problem and whether it truly is Urgent and Important. We call these your "success metrics" because if you achieve these numbers, you'll know you were successful.

3

THE FIX ➼ What are my options for solving my problem

Once you've quantified that desired future, you have to figure out how to get there. Luckily, every problem in the world has exactly three options: Do Nothing, Do It Yourself or find a Vendor. Your job here is to understand what those three options look like. This doesn't need to be a massive project, but every minute you invest upfront now will save untold dollars and time once you start spending money.

④ BUSINESS CASE ➻ I understand the options for Do Nothing, DIY, or outsource.

You need to lay out both the benefits and the costs of your options. The benefit will be the value of the success metrics you quantified in education stage. For the costs, there's more than just budget: dig deep into the initial change management effort and estimate the ongoing required maintenance. Finally, try to estimate a risk factor. What could go wrong with each approach? What would that cost? How likely is it to go wrong?

⑤ CONSENSUS ➻ My team is onboard

You might be satisfied on which way to go, but there are nine decision makers in the typical enterprise decision. You need to get all nine of those folks onboard. Each person will have different needs, priorities and perspectives, and most of them want to take the easy route and say no.

⑥ NEGOTIATE ➻ Everyone is slightly unhappy

This mostly applies if you outsourced, but if you're dealing with internal teams who are going to bill you for work, then it's the same principle. You've got to get down to a price and timeline that all participants can live with.

⑦ IMPLEMENTATION ➻ Is it live yet?

Building or buying something rarely fixes the problem just by virtue of its existence. You need to turn it on. A lot of fixes fail at launch because everyone was so focused on getting the signatures, they either didn't think about how to implement or they did the bare minimum and didn't think about the human change management.

⑧ VALUE RECEIVED ➻ Thank God I Gave You Money Day

You took a big risk to go with the approach you chose. If it had gone wrong, it would have been on you. TGIGYMD is the first day when you breathe easy because you have

proof that you backed the right horse. The problem is fixed and everyone is happy with you. It's a good day.

A couple notes

1. You can start your Buyer Journey at different points, but don't skip anything

You might start your official buying journey with one or more of these stages already complete, but if you skip any, your CFO is going to make you go back before they sign over any cash.

The main difference is if you figure out you have a problem on your own versus when a vendor brings a problem to your attention.

If you self-identify that you have a problem, then you're automatically aware and you can get straight into Education.

If you didn't know you had a problem, and just clicked on some marketing content or responded to an email, then some seller somewhere gets the job of making you aware. They'll want to educate you and move you as fast as they can through the buyers journey.

You might also just inherit a perfectly quantified problem. Great! Get to work on those Do Nothing, DIY or Get a Vendor options.

2. Working with a vendor is OK

Being a prospect isn't necessarily something to avoid. Most vendors have some expertise or insights that would help you understand your problem and they give this information away for free in the first part of the sales process. Sellers do this to establish credibility and so they can get some information about you at the same time. Having spoken to you, if they think they can

sell you something, the seller will mark you as a Prospect, they'll create an Opportunity in their CRM, and they'll start working on you.

If you're rigorous about how you go about assessing your problem and don't let yourself get sucked in, then it's to your benefit to take their input with a grain of salt and add it as just one more consideration in your decision making process.

One thing: while you don't owe sellers anything until you sign a contract, karma is a real thing.

You can make your own choices of course, but if I know beyond all doubt I'm not going to use a vendor's services, I'm upfront about that so they're not laboring under some misapprehension that I'm going to work with them. Chances are they'll still share what they know, but you can sleep easier knowing you're an ethical person.

3. The Seller's role

Assuming you're working with a vendor (rather than doing everything in-house), the Seller's job is to get you through all those buyer stages as fast as possible.

The best sellers understand that it's a waste of time to work with buyers who aren't actually going to buy anything. So they'll spend more time in the early stages to determine whether you really do have a UIP that they can help with. Then they'll spend time and energy to convince you that their solution is the best one, then they'll spend time to help you make your case to people with the money inside your organization.

The best sellers will also spend time making sure your transition from what they call "presales" (i.e. before anything is signed) to post-sale (ie: the implementation team and your long-term account manager) is smooth as silk. The smart ones will follow up one last time after implementation to make sure that you actually received the value they promised you.

Why is it that way? Either because the best sellers tend to be actually good people, or because they know that if you don't get the value they promised then they won't be able to upsell you or get a referral later. Same result to you though.

Unfortunately, the best sellers are rare. There are a lot of sellers out there who just want to hit quota and don't really care who they sell to. We'll look at how to figure out who's who in the next chapter.

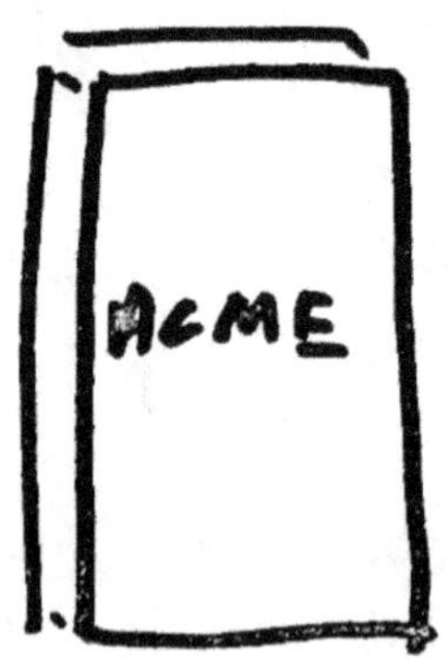

CHAPTER 1 | Sellers' Book of Tricks

Power plays and honest partners

I recognize I'm generalizing here, but if any sales book features the word 'technique,' it's probably sketchy. I say that because techniques are designed to manipulate, and true partners don't manipulate each other. We help each other and we both make money from our combined efforts. We both profit at the expense of the inefficiency, and everyone comes away better off.

I'm going to share a few of the techniques taught to sellers so you can recognize the players vs. the partners. Being on the receiving end of these techniques doesn't mean the seller is a bad person per se, but it's a flag that they might not be as helpful as they profess to be.

Don't feel bad. Over on the other side of the book, I tell Sellers about all the tricks buyers pull.

One thing to remember: You're not crazy. But you're not totally rational either. Sellers are taught over and over to appeal to your emotions because the research is clear: buying is an emotional process not a rational one. Sellers are trained to look for and exploit emotional cues. You're not going to fall for the "your job is on the line" angle, but you might seek glory if they start offering you some glory.

Deal and Value Tricks

I. **RFP "lock-in" specs** — anytime you invite a vendor to contribute to your Request for Proposal (RFP) template, they're going to add specs that they know the competitor doesn't have just to tip the RFP in their favor. The value of that spec to you is of zero concern to this seller. This is way more likely to happen if they offer you an RFP template to use with other vendors. Treat any RFP help with extreme skepticism.

II. **ROI calculator** — every ROI calculator ever has a secret multiplier in the spreadsheet someplace that makes the output equal to 10x the input. Just try and find any combination of circumstances where the calculator recommends against buying. What's the point? Use your own evaluation of reward, effort and risk so you and your CFO (and your Vendor) can evaluate your options a tiny bit more objectively.

III. **Reference customers** — you should ask to talk to a reference, but look out for vendors who always go to the same handful of references: either they don't have as many customers as they claim or they're not confident that every customer would report the glowing success they're promising you. Ask to talk to a reference who's not on the list (for example from your industry). Or even better, ask to see their customer list and scan for a name you know through your own network.

IV. **Minimizing change effort** — the ultimate sin. So many vendors downplay the effort required to get the value from their solution. Be prepared to die on this hill and don't just hope it'll all work out. Demand a mutual action plan with all the boring details.

V. **False deadlines** — vendors will say certain stages or milestones need some amount of time that they recommend. They do this to get you to move on *their* timeline, not yours. Not every deadline is a lie, but push the vendor to find out what's padding and what's real. Be very suspicious if the timing they put in front of you ends up lining up with their company's end-of- quarter (the date they have to meet their quota).

VI. **Padding statistics / results** — if you ask for examples of prior success, make sure that they're not conflating anecdotal success for statistical results. Ask when and how this stat was measured and ask them to show results from circumstances similar to your own. If you really want to make them sweat, ask to see the data and the calculation.

VII. **Misleading references** — watch for old customer names on the website or customers referencing a different part of the product than what you were asking about.

Personal Power Tricks

I. **Power grip** — people don't shake hands much anymore, but watch out for power grip people, especially men. To me, that's an almost automatic no if someone tries this stuff.

II. **Uncomfortable silence** — the sales training literature says to hold a silence and let the buyer be uncomfortable in an effort to get you (the buyer) to fill the space and start giving up intel. Two can play that game. Stay cool.

III. **Reflecting** — Rep answers the question with a question. This is also called hot potato. This lets them avoid the question you asked, and get back to them interrogating you.

IV. **Reframe** — they'll attempt to reframe your problem in a way that their solution is relevant. This is a tough one, because a good seller who has a properly informed POV will legitimately want you to look at the problem from a different angle.

V. **Liking them** — they'll try to get you to like them. It's weird. Yes, a lot of sellers are naturally charismatic, but be on guard against following their path just because they made you like them. If they say your name a lot, they probably just took the Sandler Selling course.

VI. **"That's Right"** — they affirm everything you say, then they say something totally different but pretend it's the same as your point.

VII. **Series of steps** — the idea here is to walk you down the path with a series of yes's. Easy questions at first so you get used to saying yes. Before you know it, you've agreed to something that you may not have otherwise said agreed to. It's sneaky and manipulative.

Pricing & Negotiation Tricks

I. **Price decoys** — this one is really devious. You'll be presented with several pricing options (probably as different bundles of products or differing levels of professional support), but one or more of them are not serious, they're just there to make their desired price look more appealing. For example, imagine a "Basic" at $500, "Gold" at $1000, but then "Super Platinum" at $1005. Without that Gold in there, you'd think "I should stick with Basic" but that Gold makes the Platinum look like a bargain and you go for it without thinking.

II. **Mark up to mark down** — they know the real value of their product, but they quote it high just to give themselves room to discount later. This one isn't really their fault, it's a consequence of buyer behavior and years of bad habits, with sellers knowing that buyers are going to demand a discount even for a product that is absolutely saving their bacon.

Problem
Symptom 1
Symptom 2
____
Importance $
Urgency $/month

CHAPTER 2 | **Urgent Important Problems**

Introducing DIHAP: Do I Have a Problem?

Before you get into fixes, you need to understand if you have a problem worth fixing and dig down into the root cause(s) of the problems.

If you're working with a vendor, they're going to try and push past this phase and get straight to their solution. Don't let them.

If you're doing this on your own, then recognize that the more time you spend here, the easier —and less risky— the solutioning phase will be. Measure twice, cut once. I don't have time to do it right, but I do have time to do it again.

Pick your aphorism and open up a spreadsheet.

Understanding your problem goes through five main phases

1. Do I have a problem
2. Figure out if your problem is important and urgent
3. Validate your findings
4. Figure out the root cause
5. Get a lock on what fixed looks like

I call this whole process DIHAP — "**Do I Have A Problem**"

It's really important that you do the below work with a spreadsheet. It doesn't have to be a fancy spreadsheet, but a little bit of number crunching is unavoidable here. Lean into it, and let the numbers tell their story.

You don't have to do what the numbers say, but having them at your fingertips will give you more confidence in whatever you decide.

Do I have a problem?

I split business problems into two categories: job function or industry-specific.

Job function problems are common across many types of business and industry. Think how many companies have a marketing team, HR, accounting. It could be single function like shipping or a function that spans multiple roles like a sales forecast. With function problems, it doesn't matter what your company does so much as how good your people and processes are.

Industry-specific problems are more narrow. A better drill for deep mines, specialist measurement software, a nicer hammer. Your own company likely has some special sauce to be

successful in your industry, and these are the adjacent products and services that let you do what you do better than the competition.

Regardless of the type, there are three ways you'll start to get an inkling that you may have a problem.

1 **You figure it out** — Something is taking longer than it should; something has changed in the market and now your daily operating rhythm doesn't work; you see some frustrating inefficiency in your team; you or your team isn't meeting expectations. Whatever it is, you want to get ahead of it. This is the best way to find a problem. Starting on your own means you're a thinker and it gives you a little more time to figure out severity and urgency of the problem. Note that good instrumentation covering your critical systems will make it more likely you identify problems before they cause real damage.

2 **Your boss tells you** — Your boss had the epiphany instead of you, and they asked you to figure it out. The first thing you've got to figure out here is whether the boss identified the issue on their own, or it came from *their* boss, or if it came from a vendor and the boss is kicking it down to you. If it is from the boss, in addition to figuring out if the problem is truly important and urgent, you need to figure out if your boss thinks it's urgent and important. There's every chance your boss just wants to get a vendor out of their hair. But it's also just as likely that your boss knows something you don't know, and is giving you an opportunity to shine. But politics is real, so get a lay of the land before you make your final recommendation.

3 **A vendor tells you** — It's easy to move forward with problem solving if you or your boss found the problem because you can trust their motives. But no matter how friendly they are, a vendor's first loyalty is to their company, so you just can't take their words at face value. On the other hand, what if they do know something and you ignore it? Who wins then?

A couple of notes

Vendors are more likely to offer help with function-related problems because there's a wider audience for that kind of help. Sometimes it can be hard to tell if it's an individual with a problem or a company-level problem. The best indicator is to look for what changed. If results are changing but the person is still doing the same processes that used to work just fine, then chances are the market moved beneath your feet and you got left behind. That's definitely a problem.

As you learn about this alleged problem, record where and when you come across various symptoms. It'll be so much easier later when you're making your case to colleagues. You'll also reduce your risk later on when you're thinking about solutions: you'll know what to measure and you can ensure your solution fixes all the symptoms (i.e., you successfully fixed the root cause).

One final note on problem provenance: Whether you figured out there was issue on your own or someone told you, don't look to your boss for all the answers. This is your problem to solve.

Is it important?

You've listened to your people, the symptoms are undeniable. You have a problem.

But there are a million problems in the world: problems actually worth fixing are few and far between, not least because the easy ones already got fixed.

So once you've identified enough symptoms to agree there's a problem, you need to quantify that problem. You need to figure out if it's urgent and important.

SLIGHTLY MORE EFFICIENT BUYING

Don't skip this step. You'll have to do it at some point, and if you do it now, you may well find the problem isn't as bad as you thought.

Importance as a dollar value

The universal common denominator to answering "is it important" is to figure out its cost in dollars. That's fine when it's a piece of equipment or an automated process, but a lot of problems are people problems, and those are harder to quantify.

A lot of people (and especially vendors) will convert problem importance into dollars by taking the salary of the staff impacted by the problem and just multiplying by the number of hours lost to the problem

Total Hours Lost x Average Hourly Salary = Cost of Problem.

I've never been convinced by this argument. For a start, you don't get that money back just because the employee is no longer wasting that time. Second, it's really hard to accurately quantify greater or lesser productivity of white collar professionals.

It's different if you have a labor force with time clocks and measurable outputs, but then those kinds of problems are also a lot more obvious and easier to model and test against.

If you do go down this road (maybe you're time-tracking your workers or you just know what they do all day), then consider calculating the value of the opportunity cost of that time instead of the hourly salary cost.

What valuable thing could I do with those lost hours if this resource wasn't being burned up by this problem?

If the problem is not about people or productivity, it's easier to quantify.

Let's take a look at some of those symptoms again.

In a spreadsheet, list each symptom and its dollar cost. To make the numbers meaningful, you have to include a time range for those costs to be incurred — it could be per hour, per day, per week, per quarter. Sum the value into a quarterly cost so it can be compared to other budget items.

Symptom	Cost per week per occurrence	Number of occurrences	Cost per quarter
Symptom A	$2000	200	$5,200,000
Symptom B	$100	200	$260,000
Symptom C	$5000	10	$650,000
		TOTAL COST	$6,110,000

If the number you arrive at would make your boss take a sharp breath or is bigger than any other line item in the budget, then congratulations: you have an important problem.

Now when you're prioritizing all the problems and deciding what to fix first, you have context to help you make an informed decision.

So let's prioritize it.

Is it urgent?

What kind of problem can be important but not urgent?

Urgency is just another word for prioritization. If something can wait, it's not urgent. This might be because there are higher priority projects, or you can quantify urgency of a project on its own merits by rate of change: if something is getting worse faster every day, then it's higher priority than if it's a slow bleed.

What about urgent, but not important?

These are the bane of productivity. Someone "needs" a report, or a custom part, or an answer, and they need it RIGHT NOW. Tomorrow is too late. This kind of problem comes up every day, and the binging and belling of Slack, email, DMs simultaneously popping up on desktop and buzzing your phone are literally designed to be irresistible to humans.

Ask yourself, "that thing that *needs* be done, but what if it *doesn't* get done?" Will the world end? Will the company lose $100M? Will they just ask for it again tomorrow? Will your getting distracted every 10 mins by urgent requests delay your actually important project?

Vigorously defend your team's time against other people's urgent requests. If you do take on the task, make sure those people accept the opportunity cost you're incurring on their behalf, and don't forget to include the overhead that constant context switching imposes.

But let's assume this problem is important and at least somewhat urgent.

How to prioritize a problem

Little bit of a chicken and egg here— you can't properly prioritize a problem until you're confident about the cost and change management required by the fix. But there's no point in working through the options of how to fix a problem if there are more urgent issues pressing.

But you can look at cost over time.

You already have the problem's cost over a quarter. Do a little more research to find out if the problem is stable, if it's getting better or worse on its own, and whether what's small now is just the start of something that will become catastrophic if you don't do something.

> *A leaky pipe that leaks $1000 of water per month where you've already budgeted for that amount of lost water is less urgent than a pipe at risk of suddenly bursting and gushing $10,000 a month. Sure you should fix that first pipe, but ideally you can estimate how long you can wait before it will burst and fix it right before then.*

Look at that raw number compounding every month, and decide how long you can stomach it.

Picture your CEO seeing that number six months from now and imagine the words you'd use to explain that you've known about it for while, but didn't say anything.

Finally, take that compounded number and compare it to the value of the other work you're doing. If the problem costs more than the value of what you're already doing, you have an urgent problem.

SLIGHTLY MORE EFFICIENT BUYING

Validate your UIP with an executive sponsor

At this point, you should have a list of symptoms and a spreadsheet showing some indication of scale of the problem, ideally quantified in dollars. As far as you're concerned, you've found a problem worth investigating.

But before you jump into the next step of root cause, this is a great point to check in and validate your work.

Ideally you have a good relationship with the level of leadership above you to get an informal gut check. Go to someone you trust, because if you go too high or outside your circle, you might inadvertently escalate something not necessarily worth escalating, or you might even encounter one of those jerks who say "don't bring me problems, bring me solutions."

Ping your person, emphasize that this is super early, and you just want some validation before you invest more time.

> *"Hi Jessie, do you have a minute? I've noticed some weird data that I want to check with you. Does this seem right? I did some back of envelope math on what this could be costing us. Did I miss something or is worth digging deeper?"*

In addition to validating (or poking holes in your thesis), there's a good chance Jessie will give context too, like if anyone else ever tackled this problem and how to prioritize this problem amongst all the other things other people are doing. All feedback is good. You want to learn this stuff now, not when you're in front of the CFO.

If you're successful in getting agreement that this is an important problem, then that should be enough to empower you to find a solution.

If your validator doesn't accept your DIHAP analysis, then you can either rework your angle, go get some more data to prove your point, or try a different executive sponsor.

Or there's nothing wrong with documenting your findings (by sharing your DIHAP) and moving on with your life.

Documenting and shelving is more than a CYA if your problem blows up later. A concise brief sitting and waiting at hand means that when the problem gets more urgent and more important (ie: when that pipe is getting ready to burst), or when the other higher-priority items have been handled, then you can pick up where you left off.

It is frustrating to let go of a problem because no one will listen, but I read just the other day on Reddit that knowing how to work with an incompetent boss is the key to a successful corporate life (looking at you there D.S.; Joe Wang, you're fantastic, wouldn't change a thing).

Other impacted people

It's at this point that you should start to think about other people who might be impacted by your UIP. These folks are going to be essential when you're up in front of the CFO defending your prioritization decisions and justifying all the change you're asking for.

If you don't have these relationships already, ask your executive sponsor for their best guess who would be impacted and game plan out who you should talk to to get them onboard.

SLIGHTLY MORE EFFICIENT BUYING

What about when you find a problem that's NOT your problem?

This is tough situation. If you have time to document what led you to identify the problem, then write a memo and share it with your manager. If the issue is really far out from your domain, make sure you don't burn more than an hour or so writing it up, since (a) you could well lack key information and (b) you should probably be using that time to do your own job.

If you work at the kind of place that says "stay in your lane", then consider looking for a new job. That company either has a poor internal comms or they're real insecure about their strategy.

If you find that you're consistently identifying problems that are not in your scope, then this might be a you problem. Consider finding a new company who runs the ship more in accordance with your preference or change careers and become a management consultant.

Figure out the Root Cause

You have an Urgent and Important Problem. You've documented the symptoms, it's already cost you and your company a ton, it's going to continue costing a ton, and your analysis has been validated by someone you trust.

It's so tempting to go dive in and fix those symptoms. But if you can possibly hold off and dig down a few layers, you'll be in such a better place.

Now, if the urgency is off the charts, then take the ibuprofen and stop the pain. But don't think "hey it doesn't hurt anymore, I must be cured." Pain killers give you breathing room to find the real problem. But it's borrowed time. Don't waste it.

The good news is understanding the root cause is where a great seller will stand out. A great seller understands something deeper about your business that you don't. If your vendor doesn't

have anything to offer when you ask about root cause, you're dealing with a label-reader. You can read labels just as well as they can. Expect more from your vendor: shop around til you find someone who has an interesting point of view. They're going to be more valuable in the long run, and less likely to try to get you to skip steps.

Every problem at every company is a little bit different, so I can't give you great advice on how to figure out the root cause other than say, keep asking "Why."

Dig in, ask why, dig into that, ask why again and beware of vendors who try to rush through this phase and get you on to buying their stuff.

What "Fixed" looks like

I don't think it matters which order you do Root Cause vs. What Fixed Looks Like. But if you wait til you're in solution mode before you're thinking what how you got here and what you want, then "fixed" is almost always going to end up looking like the end result of whatever solution the vendor is suggesting. It's much better to have a firm idea of what you want, then you can evaluate if the proposed solution actually hits the mark.

Sellers might talk about "future state" or what waving a magic wand would get you. Try and do this exercise without the seller's input. Even the best-intentioned seller is going to steer you towards their version of fixed.

In the software development world, engineers will talk about "User Acceptance Testing". The idea is the business owner describes what they want to be able to do as a result of a new feature, but they specifically DON'T provide detail on what that feature looks like. They purposefully leave "how" up to the engineers and product designers.

You can do the same thing here.

In the leaky pipe example, fixed means "no more water on the floor and no risk of a flood". Whether that's because you swapped out the pipe or just repaired the old one isn't part of the debate yet.

Saying something is "Fixed" doesn't mean it has to be perfect. The principle of diminishing marginal returns says that getting closer and closer to perfect gets more and more expensive.

But if you don't think about where that threshold is upfront, then you might be swayed by a vendor to go for the gold-plated pipe instead of the perfectly functional plastic one.

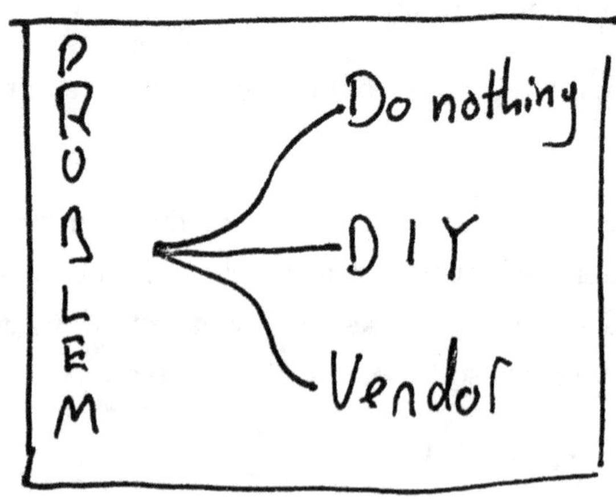

CHAPTER 3 | The Fix

You have a problem. It's important. It's urgent. You understand the Root Cause. You know more or less what the fixed future should look like.

It doesn't matter whether you figured this out on your own or with the help of a vendor. What matters now is, what are you going to do next?

You have exactly three options: do nothing, do it yourself, or get a vendor.

The next phase of your decision process is to quantify the costs and benefits of each of these three options so you can compare them objectively. You can get a ton of inputs, but at the end of this, you and you alone will be responsible for the final outcome.

I'm told there are a hundred ways to skin a cat. I don't recommend testing that, but I know what they were trying to get at: for any problem, there are multiple approaches to fixing it. And for each of those approaches, you could build or buy.

It's not reasonable to do a full analysis of every option, so you'll have to meter out some rough justice to get to a manageable short list.

Discard the obviously expensive or risky solutions. But keep them written down somewhere in an appendix to show stakeholders how you got to your top 5 and why you dumped these others. You'll look like a don when someone asks "well what about X approach" and you can say "I looked at it, but it's 10x the price so I took it out of contention. You can see the analysis here."

Before we get into the details, stick these two concepts into your memory and keep them there.

1   **Doing Nothing has Zero Opportunity Cost**

Whether you go DIY or vendor, you have limited budget and limited time. What project are you going to sacrifice to get this thing done and this problem fixed? If you opt to Do Nothing, what magic could you make with the time you would have spent on the fix? Would that deliver more value than spending the time and money on fixing your UIP? That's your opportunity cost.

2   **Value of vendor = Cost of DIY minus Cost of Vendor**

Much as the vendor would like you to believe that their value equals the value of the fixed problem, their value is actually the difference between the cost of you doing it yourself vs. whatever they're charging you. You need to work out how you'd fix this problem on your own to be able to quantify the actual value that the vendor is bringing to the table. Just try to be honest about your own capabilities.

Option 1 | Do Nothing

Before you even think about vendors, evaluate the easy choice: "do nothing".

Inaction is a lot harder to pin on someone. You're not putting your political capital on the line, you don't need to spend a bunch of time and effort evaluating and implementing something that may well not even work.

Stick to your lane. Let someone else take the heat. Maybe grab some credit at the end but otherwise keep your head down and follow protocol.

There's nothing wrong with this approach. It's natural, logical and solidly in line with human nature.

But you're not going to advance in your career by constantly laying low and avoiding decisions.

So before you hang up your spurs, run some numbers on the costs and benefits of doing nothing. This will be your reference point to evaluate the Do Something choices.

Advantages of doing nothing

1. Zero effort to implement
2. Zero change required of any team
3. Zero budget
4. Low personal risk (though this can change fast — see Costs below)
5. By saying no to this project, you open up time and money to do something potentially more valuable (opportunity cost)

Costs of doing nothing

1. You're burdened by the ongoing cost of maintaining the status quo with its urgent, important and costly problem
2. If you end up fixing the problem later, you wasted money by not doing it sooner and you might get the blame
3. If someone else evaluates the problem and finds you chose to do nothing, you might get the blame

How to calculate a dollar figure for Cost of Doing Nothing

It might seem like the cost of doing nothing is the cost of the problem. But unless fixing the problem takes zero time and zero resources, it's not quite that simple because doing nothing means you're not spending a bunch of time and effort to fix the problem. And so that time and effort can be deployed elsewhere to positive effect.

Cost of UIP - Value of opportunity cost = Cost of Doing Nothing

Opportunity cost is a really tricky subject. By its nature it has to be amorphous, because the moment you commit to a course of action, that action becomes the thing incurring the opportunity cost. In practice, don't think about the eternal spiraling, and just be explicit

> *"We're not fixing Problem X, because even though it's costing us $2M a year, if we took time & effort away from Project Y to fix it, we'd lose $3M a year. We recommend reevaluating when Project Y winds down in six months."*

In the situation where management says "actually we won't take money away from an existing project, we'll just dip into the emergency fund," it's still not simple. Instead of fixing the most

recent problem in front of you, you should revisit your shelf of Do Nothing reports (see below) and see which one has the biggest bang for this new budget that's suddenly become available and has apparently been available the whole time.

Write up your Recommendation to Do Nothing

Even though it's the right thing to do, it's actually a little bit risky to write down your rationale for doing nothing. If the Problem's profile gets raised and people find out you had the opportunity to fix it, but chose not to, you will look bad.

On the other hand, if you're advocating action and you get shot down by someone else, then writing a Do Nothing report will save you when a new problem solver comes poking around.

One thing you can do if you're overruled is add a "Return Date" to the file. Make a commitment to revisit this decision in 6 months and see if the predicted costs of the UIP actually came to pass. If the pain is worse than you expected, then rerun the effort numbers and see if you get a different result. If the pain didn't happen as bad as you predicted, you dodged a bullet. Consider seeing where you went wrong so you don't make the same bad assumption next time.

If you do decide to do nothing…

If you do decide to do nothing, be a good partner and tell the vendor. There's nothing worse than seeing a deal dry and wither over time.

Yes, they're gonna try to change your mind, but if Do Nothing is the right choice, then just be super matter-of-fact and tell them it's over. If you want to go above and beyond, you can tell them why and show them your math.

Option 2 | DIY

If Do Nothing is too expensive to bear, then you have to Do Something.

For each Something, start by working out how you'd do it yourself. This not only lets you see if you can fix it real quick, but it'll also give you a baseline from which to understand exactly what each vendor is bringing to the table.

But you don't need to do this pre-work in isolation. The vendor wants to help, so let them, because they might know something you don't. Just make sure you remember their motivations and keep that grain of salt handy.

My favorite question to ask a vendor is this:

> *"How would I fix this if I didn't have your solution?"*

I like this because a single question lets you evaluate how authentic your rep is and how much domain knowledge they really have.

They'll have to dig a little deeper and stop positioning their solution as this magic box where you stick a $10 bill in one end and a $20 comes out the other side. They'll have to explain how their solution solves the problem.

Worst case you learn that your vendor doesn't know much. Best case you get some helpful insights into how you'd do it in-house.

Whether you're doing this on your own, or with a vendor, let's look at the steps required to understand the approach, effort and risks of DIY.

Write a brief

The worst thing you can do at this point is launch into prototyping a solution. The more time you spend upfront thinking through the issues, the less re-work you'll have to do. Think deeply. Use a whiteboard and imagine what should happen in outlier scenarios.

If you write a design brief, then it's easy to share your thinking with others, and if you do move forward, then you have a blueprint for your work.

This can be in deck form or a word doc, or a set of Agile stories. Just capture your idea in a way that can be shared & evaluated by others.

Here's a list of all the things to think about. I'm going deep on purpose because building real, reliable solutions (be it software, hardware or a new business process) is a totally different level of effort compared to knocking up a quick proof of concept.

- Summarize your UIP analysis, especially the root cause of the problem
- Summarize how your fix will work in 30-50 words
- List the main workflows that users will run through
- List the major 4-5 milestones for development, deployment and training. Then for each milestone list out
    - How will you know you did it successfully?
    - Where is data coming from and how does it sync?
    - Who needs to do work or sign off (and are they onboard)?
    - What's the milestone's expected duration?
    - What are the risks / what's most likely to go wrong / how are you mitigating?
- What is the overall timeline?
- What is the budget?
- What is the in-house effort: New vs. repurposed / proprietary vs off-the-shelf?

If this is software, comp out some UI wireframes. Wireframes make communicating ideas so much easier, and make it so much easier to mentally walk through the app in search of logical traps or user dead ends. If you skip the wireframe, then I guarantee that the people you're working with will be imagining something completely different than what you're thinking.

If you're running this DIY experiment in parallel with vetting a vendor, then ask your vendor for their mutual action plan for evaluating and implementing their solution. It won't show all the detail of actually building the insides of the solution, but you will see which people and process they intend to impact. Then you can make sure to account for the same in your brief.

2 Include onboarding & ongoing support & maintenance

The last 20% of any project takes 80% of the work. So you probably *could* build your own solution — or at least a proof of concept, 80%-of-the-way fix. And if you're the only person impacted by the problem, then a hacky DIY job might be all you need.

But cast your mind back to a time when you built a spreadsheet to solve a problem. You built the app and it worked for a few weeks, but then it started spitting out bad data. You can always find the issue: a broken connector, a bad lookup, an updated or deprecated dependency. But if you added up the time, you end up spending more effort maintaining these spreadsheets than it took to build the first version.

That's exacerbated exponentially when other people start using your app. Now it NEEDS to work, and they don't know the tricks of when to refresh a manual import or which column to never ever edit.

You can support a handful of colleagues on an ad hoc basis, answering questions (probably answering the same questions over and over), helping with stupid stuff like logins, but when you get a larger teams, you need to invest in proper support.

That doesn't necessarily mean hiring support people, but it does mean good self-serve documentation for onboarding and ongoing use.

Vendors have documentation and training materials. Perhaps more important, they have people financially motivated to make your colleagues use the app properly. If you DIY a solution, then be prepared to also DIY support, training, weekend calls and budget time not just for maintaining the software, but fielding feature requests (and probably adding new features as a result).

3 Get it validated

Go back to your UIP analysis and pretend for a moment that your design is a vendor proposal. Are you actually fixing the root cause or just papering over the symptoms?

Ask the people who helped you validate the urgent important problem to take a look at your brief as if you'd just given it to them to implement.

What detail would be missing for them to execute the blueprints? That's the detail that will end up jacking you and making you wish you'd never started.

Remember, this DIY exercise will have payoffs even if you end up going with a vendor. You have your baseline and now you're ready to compare with what a vendor can do for you.

Option 3 | Go with a Vendor

The obvious advantage to going with a vendor is they specialize in this problem, so they probably know more than you. But the real reason is that you know something special too — that secret sauce that makes you better than your competitor.

If you want to stay competitive, you need to focus on your domain knowledge — honing it, adding distance to the gulf between you and your competitors. Reinventing the wheel rather than just buying the perfectly good tire from Les Schwab eats up your innovation budget. You may save some money short term, but long term you're just doing the operations parts of your business slightly worse than if you bought a solution, all with a fatal opportunity cost to whatever you actually specialize in.

So assuming you're serious, then the main criteria for a vendor are credibility and capability.

Can I trust this vendor?

First, remember that a vendor is so much more than their sales rep. You can have an untrustworthy rep working for a trusted company, and while it's less likely, you can have a good rep working for a bad company. Neither scenario lasts for long, but you could get caught out.

Second, when I say untrustworthy, I don't mean actual liars. I'm differentiating between those sellers who believe that the path for their own long term prosperity is fixing customers problems versus those thinking shorter term who just want to win as many deals as possible, irrespective of customer need or value.

Trust and credibility are built up over time, but you can short-cut the process by flying close to the sun and asking uncomfortable questions about capability.

Is what they're offering worth paying for?

There are lots of different types of seller. Reps with strong domain knowledge may have been a sales engineer or even a practitioner before they took on a sales role, but these folks might lack project management skills and communication skills needed to apply complex concepts to your specific situation. Of course, the best sellers are expert in both domain and soft skills. As the buyer, you'll need aspects of both at different times during the buying process.

Ask yourself, "would I pay a consultant for this advice and project management support?"

Here are a couple questions to figure out what kind of sales rep you're working with.

1

Ask about Root Cause

"Without talking about your product, can you explain what's going on in my business that's causing these problems? Peel it back for me". The opportunity for trust building is that you made a specific ask to not talk product. Any seller who is serious about fixing problems will leap at the opportunity to diagnose your root cause issues independent of potential solutions. Can they honor your request? Do they actually know something? Are they able to communicate that insight to you in a way you understand?

2

Ask them what their competition does well

A smart seller will build credibility by acknowledging that they don't do everything 100% best in the world. Because no one does. Look for a seller who is self-aware enough —and confident enough — to acknowledge areas of weakness. Look for authenticity where the thing that they say the competitor does well is actually important. If they try and blow you off with a joke, let them know you're serious. If they really don't know the competition, then they don't have the domain expertise they claim.

3 Ask to talk with an implementation specialist

Remember, you're not dealing with just one sales rep, so don't be afraid to engage deeper into the org to find out if this org and this rep can be trusted. You're looking to see if these other people give the same answers that your rep gave.

So who to talk to?

Implementation people know where the bodies are buried and are less likely to hide the truth. About midway through your education phase, ask to speak with the person who'd be managing your implementation. Include a technical or operations person on your team who'd be involved so they ask some detailed questions. This is a good intro for peer-to-peer contacts that can get stuck deals unstuck later in the process.

I like to ask about implementation time frame and where risks to a smooth go-live like to hide. Like the competitor question, honest answers about where things can go wrong demonstrate both integrity and a degree of self-awareness and confidence that only capable people have.

One thing: Implementation people are in high demand, so make it clear you only want a short call and that you're not asking for work from them at this point, just asking about process so your own team can prepare properly.

4 Ask to see a path

"Don't tell me you're funny; make me laugh."
Saying "Trust me" is the least credible thing a seller — or anyone — can say to engender trust. Instead, a good seller will share a detailed plan of how you could work together.

SLIGHTLY MORE EFFICIENT BUYING

Note the "could". Don't let the seller dictate timeline and milestones. You need to own the list of things that need to be done. The vendor can advise, and you should listen, (albeit with that grain of salt) but this is your timeline and your project.

A question to ask here is "what is driving these timeline assumptions?," A good seller will run with this and dig into the mechanics of fixing your problem, proving their expertise.

Make sure that their path goes all the way to Thank God I Gave you Money Day. If it ends at signatures, take that as a sign that your seller is not as focused on fixing your problem as they claim.

5 Ask your friends

Saving the most obvious and most important one for last — references.

Sellers will always prefer to share a case study rather than make an intro reference. It's not sinister. It just slows down the deal, adds an element of risk as the rep can't be sure what the reference will say, and costs the seller some political capital having to ask their current customers for the favor of their time.

On your end, if you get a cold reference, it's impossible to know if they're giving you the full picture. They obviously like the vendor and they're been thoroughly vetted, so who knows how much they're brushing under the carpet.

It's WAAAAY better if you know the reference personally. So ask the seller for a customer list, and see if there's a company you already know. Then reach out directly. You'll get the most honest answer possible. Promise your friend anonymity and you'll get an even more direct response.

CHAPTER 4 | The Decision

Collaborating on the gritty stuff to get to a decision

You've got a problem. It's urgent. It's important. You understand the root cause. You've worked through the pros and cons of doing nothing, of fixing the problem yourself or finding a partner. You've had some light validation from colleagues as you worked through all these things.

If it was just up to you, you know which way to go and you're confident your decision is the path most likely to fix the problem and make the world a better place. Assuming the answer was not "do nothing", you'd just click your fingers and get to work.

But if this problem is anything bigger than where to have lunch, it's not just up to you.

You need to get consensus across your team, adjacent teams, ops, IT, legal, leadership and Finance. You need to win budget (both financial and people resources). You need to nail down that hanging 20% of detail that always waits to the last minute.

If you opted to go with a vendor, you need to negotiate a final price and timeline, statement of work, service level agreements, and get a contract or order statement drafted, redlined and signed.

If you didn't go with a vendor you still need to negotiate a lot of these with your internal resources, and you should still write it down so everyone is operating on the same gameplay, you just may not need to get signatures.

Remember for everything past this point in your buying process, you need to expand beyond the scope of your problem and enter the bigger pond of your entire company, because that time, attention and budget that you need is in high demand from people who have absolutely no interest in your problem, or at least are nowhere near as invested as you are.

To get to a decision, you need four things

1. Consensus within your company
2. Budget from somewhere
3. Compelling business case
4. Legal sign off

Let's dig into each one, then wrap it up with some negotiation and 11th hour checks.

Internal consensus: who do you need on your side?

The basic flow goes like this

1. Understand your org's power structure
2. Figure out who's on your side and understand why
3. Figure out who's against you, and understand why
4. Figure where you stand amongst all of that human messiness
5. Try not to fling up your hands and quit

If you don't take the time to build this consensus coalition, you're going to hit a brick wall the moment you try and step outside of your team or department.

Coalition building is frustrating. The people involved each have their own point of view and personal ambitions running through the decision matrix like lightning lines, so you can't just rely on logic to carry your point. Those same people don't like making decisions or commitments. It's risky for them. If they end up on the wrong side of a decision, they lose face or worse. If someone endorses you, they're using up political capital for something that might go wrong.

Just like it would have been easier for you to Do Nothing, it's 10x easier for these others, since it's not even their problem. For several of the buying team, it's just going to be more work with literally no benefit to them personally.

Try to keep all this in mind when you're designing your business case by making sure you show how the fix is going to impact the person you're talking to. And be patient: it's not their problem, and they're giving up something to even spend 30 minutes listening to you.

Your Tiger Team

You might hear a vendor refer to this as the Buyer Committee — it's the people who will make the decision.

It's funny, but at this stage, you're in a very similar boat to a vendor. You're trying to sell a change. You might not know who makes decisions, or how those decisions get made. It's even harder when your company is going through change or being buffeted by external events, since the decision makers themselves might not know either.

But at least you're on the inside. Start with the people in your org you trust. These are the folks you already did a gut-check with. They recognize you have an urgent important problem, and they at least nominally support the fix you've arrived at. Then build out from there.

Approach the below personas one at a time with a goal to get them to the first meeting to hear your problem and evaluate your proposed fix. This doesn't need to be a massive production, just say something like this

> *I'm putting together a tiger team to validate my analysis of [your urgent & important problem] and make a decision on how we should solve it. I understand you helped with [something similar] last year. That made a real impact [what] and I think this is similar, so your input would be super helpful. Can you read this one page brief and attend one meeting? X, Y, Z are already in.*

Later on in the process, you'll want a firmer commitment from your stakeholders, but in the early phase, it's a very light touch.

Let's dig into the profiles of the people you need on your tiger team. Keep in mind that each of these roles may well require more than one actual person — the typical buyer committee has 7-12 people for a large enterprise buying / resourcing decision.

Executive sponsor

This is a person quite senior in your org who can get things done. They don't need to be your friend; for your purposes they just need a track record of shepherding similar projects to (successful) completion. They don't need to be in the C-suite, though that doesn't hurt. When they talk, other people in the org listen. They think bigger than their own job security. They are personally ethical and you can take them at their word. Don't be fooled here. A LOT of people have believed an exec who says "sure I'll back you" only to find out they were being polite, or they don't have the time or energy or even the real political power you need to get change.

Be explicit in what you're asking for, and show them your buying team members. Get their insights regarding the profiles you're targeting and whether you have the right people fulfilling those roles.

Technical Decision Maker & FP&A

Who is the CFO going to tap to evaluate your root cause analysis and your recommended fix? This can't be your buddy in IT. You need the person the CFO trusts. They might delegate someone else for the day-to-day, but your tiger team needs a representative from your IT or Financial Planning & Analytics team.

End users

Your CFO will want to hear from end-users. That they agree with the problem, with the fix, and that they've signed up for the change you want to see.

Your Detractors

Any detractors' opposition is probably nothing to do with you personally or your UIP, and everything to do with opportunity cost your project imposes on *their* projects or personal advancement (or personal time). But knowing it isn't personal doesn't save your project.

Some detractors won't tell you what they're thinking to your face, but unless you work at a horrible company where backstabbing is encouraged, they're unlikely to tell you an outright lie.

If you're meeting resistance from one of the stakeholders, try to look at the bigger picture beyond the scope of your problem and ask them to share their perspective.

It's really important that you make the effort to understand their point of view. First, they might have a legitimate point. Maybe there is another project that's 10x more important than your project that needs their time before yours. Maybe they know something about a tangential system that will need a ton of extra work you hadn't figured into your fix.

Ask them "are there any other factors we should be considering?"

Write down what you've heard and share it back, "Did I capture your concerns fairly here?"

Add their opposing POV into your business case. Tell them you're doing it, and ask them to back up their POV with data so you can include it in the equation.

In addition to legitimate points, there's also laziness. There are people in the world who will say "it can't be done" then they actually mean "I can't be bothered to figure out if it can be done" or "I don't want to do it".

Asking for data for your business case will separate the wheat from the chaff.

Do watch out — just because you caught a lazy person without data to back up their detraction does not magically convert them into a proponent for your plan.

How a vendor can help

You don't need to do all this consensus building yourself. Your vendor should be tripping over themselves to help.

They've done this before, so they should have a good sense of which roles are needed when for a successful rollout and adoption. Work with the vendor to understand these roles, then you can figure out who fills those roles at your org.

A good vendor will know what work is required across your org to implement the fix. They should have content that quantifies the timeline, effort and risks of implementation. They should also be able to explain not just the effort, but also the benefits that come to each stakeholder from implementing the fix.

Yes your vendor can help - but you need to keep control

Just remember, vendors are like fire: a good servant but a cruel master.

With even the best of the best, their goal is to control the direction of the conversation towards buying their stuff, so use them in all of the below work, but keep some dynamic tension in place and don't let go of the steering wheel.

The vendor will be working hard to build out an org chart of your decision makers. They're doing this because reps know there are multiple decision makers, and they know that having relationships with all those people makes it more likely that they'll win the deal. In the lingo it's called multithreading and it's one of the best indicators of deal health.

A good compromise is showing who's involved on both sides of the deal, with a visual representation of the peer-to-peer relationships across the buying team and selling team. This will boost your confidence in the fix, and make it easier for your other decision makers to see that all the bases are covered.

Your vendor will be pushing to meet folks higher up in the power structure. They want to meet your boss. This can be a good thing once you've decided that this is the vendor you want.

One tactic vendors use is to ask for a 10 minute meeting with you and the decision maker so the vendor can hear any concerns first hand. They'll ask you "what are some of the questions your decision maker might ask that we need to be ready for, let's ask them"

A good vendor will ask insightful questions that demonstrate their value as a partner.

At the end of the day, this is a great soft test of which direction your leadership is leaning, and a good way to see how well vendor performs under pressure, *BEFORE* your job is on the line.

How to find budget

It's simply not true when someone says "there's no budget". Unless your company is literally broke, there's budget. What they mean is "there's no budget for your project".

But of course there isn't. Why would there be? No one thought you needed to fix this problem back when you didn't know it existed. Back before you knew it was urgent and important and had a root cause that was imposing real damage. But could be fixed with low risk.

There are four ways to get budget for a project.

1. Wait until budget planning season
2. Reallocate budget from existing project(s) to the new project
3. Pull from secret magic general purpose fund
4. Get the project to pay for itself

Wait for budget season

This is the easiest approach, and just as you presented the pros and cons of "Do Nothing" in your Fix analysis, you should include the orderly, in-cycle option as the default to beat.

Is your urgent important problem really so urgent that you need to change course on a different project? Is it worth the disruption and the political fight? Your DIHAP (Do I ave A Problem) Cost Spreadsheet should answer that: "Waiting til January will cost $25M" If you're not confident in your DIHAP numbers, then you should strongly consider waiting.

Reallocate existing budget

You want this problem solved now? Get money from somewhere else.

If there's budget that you control, then this is a LOT easier than yoinking money from someone else's project. If you don't have budget, then it's not on you to decide which project gets deprioritized. It's probably not that wise to even make the suggestion.

Let your business case do the talking. Show how important this problem is, and let the CFO's office do the math on which existing project is less important. If you have tight numbers and a solid endorsement from colleagues all wrapped up in a business case, then you'll easily elbow out the projects that got green-lit from the back of an envelope.

Pull from the secret magic fund

Yes, there is a secret slush fund. No, you probably don't have access to it. Emergency budgets are for emergencies.

Now if your DIHAP shows a massive massive urgent problem, or if the cost is negligible in the grand scheme, then it's a different story, but your CFO will be looking at all the other options before tapping the strategic reserve.

Again, this will be a decision that your CFO makes when you're asking for budget. Your responsibility ends at providing good data for the CFO to make the call.

Get the project to pay for itself

This is the win-win scenario that every vendor will promise. Fixing the problem will deliver so much additional money that the project pays for itself.

The problem is every ROI ever made has over-represented the return and minimized the investment. And even if the ROI calculation was accurate, you need budget to get the return before you can spend it.

The only way this can work is to start small

1. Break out the smallest possible unit of work and implement it
2. Use the money that's saved from that first go-around to pay for the second unit of work

You can continue to sow-and-reap, sow-and-reap on these micro-implementations (although you might find that you can stop short of a full implementation and get disproportionate value) or you can go back to the CFO with data that any budget you "borrow" will be returned with high confidence on a known timeframe.

But the fact is, this pay for itself thing is tough and takes a long time.

Legal

I did a parachute jump once. As you can imagine, the liability waiver was quite substantial.

I actually started to get nervous waiving away all the various ways this jump could go bad until getting to the clause that read "I am aware I might land on a venomous snake", and I realized I was reading the creative imaginations of someone who was paid by the word.

Legal is a surprising time suck, even on the simplest thing. Their job is to think of every single thing that could possibly go wrong.

The big insight I had dealing with legal is that their job is to highlight all the things that *could* go wrong, NOT make the final decision on what to do.

You can negotiate with them for which of their concerns need to be explicitly added into the contract versus those for which you just say "thank you, your concern is taken under advisement".

If you try and include everything they mark up, at the very least you'll massively delay your project (adding to the cost of your urgency) or at worst your vendor could walk and you're left with an urgent and important problem burning away.

You might need to escalate to a more senior representative in your legal team to accept your "thanks, but no thanks" as junior legal counsel may not have the risk management experience to know what's OK to leave aside, even if technically it could possibly possibly come true.

Wrap it all up with a bow on top: the business case

It might sound like more trouble than it's worth — and it will certainly *feel* like it's more trouble than it's worth at times — but a business case is going to be your best friend.

Think of the business case as the means, not the ends.

The process of writing down your case will force you to think of all the issues that your CFO will ask about. It will sharpen your point of view so you can defend your thesis to the CEO. It'll show your vendors that you're a serious player. It will help your implementation team understand what they should focus on achieving.

Months from now it will help you (and those you've empowered) make decisions faster and more autonomously and will help you evaluate the project as a whole much more objectively.

Finally, if you can make a good business case, you will rise through the ranks faster. The written word is more durable than a meeting, so when your business case gets forwarded, leaders will see you're thoughtful, deliberate and rational. Those are good attributes to be known for.

Business case rubric

1. Keep it short - no more than 5 minute read
2. Keep it real - use people's names and real dates and as much real data as possible
3. Make it yours - don't rely on your vendor. Put it in your font, on your paper, in your name

Business Case Table of Contents

As for the actual content, remember you've already done most of the work for the below

Executive Summary

1 I like to write this first before I start to gather the other components. It helps me focus my point and I can check the other parts are all in support of my thesis. Figure this is the only section that many of your decision makers will actually read, so include the names of the people on your tiger team and promise that they've endorsed the contents.

2 **The Problem**

Summarize your DIHAP urgent & important problem analysis plus a section on the Root Cause analysis. Ideally you can put this into the context of a published company goal so it's easier for the reader to categorize & prioritize the problem.

3 **The Solution**

Summarize DIY and Vendor options to show you've done the thinking. Then share your recommendation.

4 **Implementation Plan**

Summarize major milestones on a timeline, including the people / teams needed for each. Make sure you highlight the date first value is expected.

5 **Impact analysis**

Who will be impacted positively? Who has to do work to make this happen? Again, you already worked this out in the DIHAP, just write it down.

6 **Risks**

What could go wrong and how are you mitigating. Be honest and don't hide stuff. If someone else identifies a risk that you didn't address, you've blown all credibility.

7 **Success Looks Like**

How will you know you've been successful?

8 **Financial Analysis**

CFOs don't want the full blow-by-blow value prop. In the first 7 seconds they're going to decide whether or not give you an additional 30 seconds, then they're going to check your proposal against a standard rubric of what it takes to get blood out of the stone.

This'll be the same for approving allocation of internal resources or allocating budget for an external vendor.

With this in mind, add a page or a slide at the top of your deck specifically for the CFO.

Here's the checklist the CFO will be using

- ☐ This project furthers one or more of our current objectives, and the key result is measurable.
- ☐ The budget includes implementation & ongoing cost.
- ☐ We're not buying shelfware: There is a thought out implementation & adoption plan.
- ☐ The project owner has addressed dependencies & impact on every dept in the company, both for implementation and ongoing support.
- ☐ There is a low-risk, fast way to ascertain value before we commit a lot of money or time.
- ☐ Either the project owner or the vendor has provided a reference customer I can talk to.

Deck or Doc?

Creating your business case as PowerPoint / Slides deck or a written document depends on your company culture. Look at how your executive staff crank out key documents like business plan, board notes, marketing strategy etc.

Deck advantages are easier placement of supporting graphs or graphics, and there's organic pressure to keep each section to a single slide. The disadvantage is it's difficult to demonstrate deep thinking on that single slide. If you do opt for deck, be sure you add a manual table of contents and include an appendix with all the details for later reference.

Docs allow for more thinking, but there's a very high risk your reader will drown in detail. With docs it's harder to skim a quick read or jump around to different sections. If you opt for doc, be consistent in your headers and formatting so readers know what they're looking at.

My personal opinion is that decks go out of date a lot faster, and unless you put a bunch of effort in, you might get dinged for poor design even if your business case is sound.

Negotiating

There are whole books on this. But here are a few tips about what the seller is thinking that should help you negotiate on price. I'm sharing this to get everyone on the same page, not for you as a buyer to nail your rep to the wall. Be fair. Be good.

Where are you in the month / quarter / year

Sellers live and die by quarterly results. Their pay is based on it. Their team's entire evaluation is based on hitting their quarterly target. It's even more important at year end. As you get closer to end-of-quarter, reps will be increasingly motivated to close a deal. This is good and bad. Good in that you have more leverage to play hardball. Bad in that they're going to be less likely to have your long term best interests in mind, and thus more likely to pressure you or recommend you buy unnecessary stuff.

Price Levers

Trading price for longer contracts or faster payment isn't the same as straight discounting because the seller is getting something in return for the discount. Higher volume, case study or referral commits, new industry penetration are also common levers. And of course timing, as described above. But I hate that one. It's ugly.

"Just Because" Discounting

Many companies build some buffer into pricing so reps can give Procurement their pound of flesh. Most reps can offer a 6-12% discount without getting approval from their deal desk (aka the Finance / Legal team sitting inside a selling org responsible for negotiating deals).

Personal note: "just because" discounting always makes me sad. When a seller discounts, it tells me either they were trying to rip me off on the first proposal or they don't really believe their value promise.

Net net: until everyone has read this book and becomes *slightly more efficient*, it pays to just ask for a discount.

Final Commitments: Money, Time and People

Once you sign on the dotted line, you lose a lot of power. So before you take out your pen, get everything else you want dialed in and agreed in writing.

Projects get done by people and work happens on calendars.

Before anyone can make the final Go/No Go decision, you need to be crystal clear that the right people are available when you need them. You probably identified many of these people during your internal consensus building, but now that the rubber is hitting the road and you need to time commitments for specific dates, you'll find that the earlier abstract "sure that sounds good" may not turn into a firm date-driven commitment without a little effort.

This applies to the people inside your org just as much as it applies to any vendor.

Implementation plan

Every vendor has an A-Team of implementation specialists. They also have guys that they've been meaning to fire, only they're too busy to find replacements. Before you sign, find out where you rank and who they're planning on assigning to your implementation.

- Is your implementation window guaranteed, or are you just added to the back of a queue?
- By what criteria will they select your Account manager and Customer Success manager?
- Will that person be dedicated or is it a pooled resource?
- How many other accounts is that person responsible for?
- How will the sales team be packaging up your problem and solution so the post-sales team can hit the ground running?

Get it in writing with dates

You have to this commitment before you sign, because once that pen hits the paper, it's really hard to get favorable changes.

To get commitments you can rely on, you need a timeline. It can be part of the mutual action plan you run with your vendor, it can be an internal spreadsheet, doesn't really matter, as long as something is managing who you need when, and everyone can see it.

The people need to see when you need them and they need to see that others are relying on the work they'll do. They need to see their commitment is public. They need to see that their managers see the commitment and have signed off on it.

So get it in writing and make it public.

SLIGHTLY MORE EFFICIENT BUYING

11th Hour Decision Checklist

If you're going with a vendor, then a couple days before you sign, review this list one more time so you're confident in your decision. Score 1-5 or just Yes/No. Keep it with the business case.

1 **Do nothing , DIY or outsource**

Did you learn anything since you made your outsource decision to warrant revisiting? Maybe the Vendor soft-pedaled the amount of change management earlier, and as you're closer to signing, some more truth has slipped out, or some other department just announced a massive project that's going to take resources you'd earmarked for your own implementation.

2 **All detractors heard**

Is someone in your org going to say they weren't consulted or stymie implementation out of spite? Fix it before you spend the money.

3 **Timeline**

Confirm with the vendor that the implementation dates AND the time to value dates are locked in. This includes knowing who's doing what on their side and your side. This really should be written down in the mutual action plan.

4 **Verifiable outcomes**

You know what success should look like and you have a mechanism and a timeline in place to say objectively "success or failure".

Everything look good? Get out the pen and pop the champagne because your urgent and important problem is about to go away.

Post Decision Retrospective

You've signed the deal (or got the sign-off for your DIY approach). You're feeling good and anxious to get to implementation.

But you've learned a lot during this process of identifying, prioritizing and fixing your urgent and important problem. It really shouldn't go to waste.

You learned how your company makes decisions and deals with change. You learned which coworkers you can trust and which ones are lazy. Ideally you've learned something about yourself too, your strengths and weaknesses and what makes you an effective operator.

Write down some notes right now while it's all still fresh.

Take a look at your original timeline, and compare expectation with reality. Try not to wince at your naivety and fresh-faced hopefulness on how long stuff takes.

☐ Did any process (legal, security, CFO approval) take longer or shorter than expected?
☐ Did any people pop out unexpectedly and demand a voice at the table?
☐ Did the CFO ask for anything that you hadn't expected they'd want to see?
☐ Did anyone leave you hanging? Did anyone go above and beyond and save your bacon?
☐ Did you enjoy the game or was this just super stressful?
☐ Did you lose your temper or lose hope at any stage? What got you back?

Right now, these notes are just for you. So get it all down, good bad and ugly and we'll make a sanitized version later.

All done?

Go take a sip of that champagne. Nice work :)

CHAPTER 5 | Make it Happen

How to ensure a smooth implementation

Whether you're going DIY or vendor, the key to successful implementation is a rock-solid kickoff and an iron clad schedule that includes regular public reporting up to power.

That executive awareness will minimize the risk of your project getting deprioritized to oblivion and give you the ability to get stuck things unstuck.

You can skip this chapter if you're just buying commodities or hardware that has zero training or implementation. Frankly I'm surprised you read of any this book at all.

If you go with a vendor, then as soon as you sign the contract, there's a very important shift in the power dynamic. While the selling team's anxiety drops from maximum overdrive down to zero, your anxiety will go from medium high to near max. You want results to prove that you made the right decision. They just want to be done and onto the next one.

Fixing an urgent and important problem goes through four stages after the final GO decision:

- ☐ Implementation
- ☐ Rollout
- ☐ First value
- ☐ Thank God I Gave You Money Day

These four stages apply whether you're doing DIY or vendor; the only difference is who's thanking who at the end.

A moment of advocacy praising mutual action plans

As the founder of the company that first stuck mutual action plans on the web, I feel like I've been really restrained so far in this book extolling the virtues of well documented buyer/ seller collaboration.

A mutual action plan is a set of milestones agreed by both parties for how to fix a problem. It tracks who needs to do what and then they when they need to do it. They're valuable because as a buyer, you've probably never bought a solution from this vendor to fix this problem, and as a vendor, they've probably never run something through your buying process.

So both of you know about 60% of what you need to know to make this thing happen. The mutual action plan is the spot to connect that knowledge so all the stakeholders on both sides know what they need to know.

Mutual action plans are really useful to stop deals getting stuck in the mud, and lots of sales teams use them to get a deal over the line. But the real value is actually post-signature when you the buyer want to get things implemented and rolled out.

Before you sign anything, demand a written plan from implementation through problem solved, with dates, who's involved, and what success looks like for each milestone.

This could come from your vendor, or if you're DIY, you owe one to your team.

Implementation

The implementation milestone is bound by a kick off call sometime after the contract (or internal sign-off) and a go-live date.

After the kickoff call, the technical team will start to plug stuff in, configure it, and integrate it into existing systems. The more you prep for this stage, the fewer things will go wrong, but it's inevitable that something will slip past you and you'll encounter a team or system that you didn't think would be impacted, but turns out is a blocker.

Build in some padding for these unknown unknowns, otherwise you'll be starting on the back foot with a late project and a bad taste in the mouth before anyone has even tried to see if your fix really fixes your urgent and important problem.

If you're working on a mission-critical business process, then you should require the implementation team to have a test plan to make sure everything is working as expected before anything goes live. Ideally the implementation team is doing a dry run in an environment that's as close to production as possible (known as a sandbox). Even with a sandbox in place, look for a reliable roll-back procedure just in case the worst happens.

If you want, you can ask annoying questions like "what happens to data flowing into the system during the cut-over from old system to new?" or "can you actually reverse a database migration, or are you just using a backup, and what happens to the data generated since that backup was made?"

Go Live doesn't necessarily mean people are using the solution at that exact moment, it just means everything is ready to go. There should be a final check before you give the go-live order, and business should be the one giving the order, not the technical team, especially if it's a hard cut-over from old to new.

Rollout

Where implementation is building the car, rollout is throwing the gearbox into first and heading out into the great outdoors. Unless your fix is completely behind the scenes and no one will ever interact with it (or see any knock-on effects), then you need a rollout plan.

Remember how we said change management is what makes or breaks projects? Well implementation is the easy part. It's a technical process ruled by a checklist, with each item checked off as done or not done. Implementation is peanuts compared with getting people to actually use something they're not familiar with.

Rollout is about the people. And that means that in addition to practical training, you'll need to plan on some re-selling as well.

Selling from scratch

Not all the people on the receiving end of your fix will have been involved in the run up to rollout. If you dive straight into training, then you face a strong probability of active revolt or at least passive noncompliance. So plan on some sizzle before you get into the steak.

Obviously, if you have a vendor, they'd seem like a natural for this role, except that your people don't know or trust your vendor. Smarter is to have internal advocates who've already been using the fix for a while testify their experience (we'll talk about where to find these early adopters in the next section).

Your "sales pitch" should be a more upbeat version of your business case. So just like you did there, show the nature of the problem, the cost it was imposing and a little bit of root cause for credibility. Then bring in your ringers to lay it on a little thicker for how the fix is going to make everything better. Close by highlighting the people on your tiger team so the troops know senior leadership is onboard and that this idea has been well vetted.

The selling might be easy. If your urgent and important problem renders obvious pain onto folks, then they'll be keen to change. But chances are those problems were fixed ages ago, and now you're working on the tougher problems that don't have easy answers.

Some fixes require work. These are the hardest kinds of solutions to rollout, because you're asking for permanent change, not just a temporary blip.

In these cases, double down on selling. Show why this is important, and for God's sake, figure out some angle where the change benefits the poor sods upon whose shoulders the burden of your amazing fix will rest.

Be honest about the amount of work the change will require, because any information gaps you create will be filled with guesses, which normally trend to worse-than-real. If your rollout requires a lot of time, make a point of removing some other duty so your team doesn't feel like it's just more more more.

Perception is huge in this early phase. If they see the benefit of the fix — especially if there's benefit to themselves — people will be a lot more likely to put in the effort. This perception of "worth it" is also why we'll talk about a first value / quick win in a minute.

Skills training

As for the actual training, the easiest route is to take advantage of your existing People team or enablement team and fold your training into a master company training schedule. Show the team the problem and the change of behavior you want and work with them as the experts for how to make it happen in your organization. By all means, introduce the vendor.

If you go this route, then make sure that team is represented in your 11th Hour Committed Checklist, otherwise you risk getting to launch time only to hear Enablement doesn't have time to do anything til next quarter because they don't want to overburden the team.

Personally I find this maddening. But People and Enablement don't care about your urgent and important problem. They don't care about those leaky pipes. So it's easy to say "let's just wait".

So sometimes you have to go around them.

If it looks like your formal training channels are unavailable, then consider a roadshow or "guest star in a box" where you and the vendor get on the agenda of the team meetings of the people you need to educate.

Get a 10-15 minute slot and spend 80% on selling, and 20% showing the rollout plan, including level of effort.

If you can't win time for a proper onboarding session after that (where by the way you do the selling bit all over again) then make a set of 3-4 10 min videos and get a commitment from the first line managers that their team will watch. Be public in tracking completion percentages.

If you went with a vendor, then lean on them heavily for the training materials, but make sure all the content is oriented towards fixing your problem, not just a generic spray of everything their software can do. That means more work for the vendor to customize their standard deck.

Be ok with that and make sure they are too. It could make the difference between success and crushing annihilation of your career prospects.

Roll out strategies

You might not have a choice on roll out strategy. Your fix might be a hard switch-over that means the old way of doing things is gone. The problem might be so important and urgent that you need everyone onboard as fast as possible. But ideally you have a little bit of a window.

Early Adopter / Soft launch

Recruit a cohort of early adopters. Stack the deck and choose people who you trust to give it a good shot and are most likely to do well. Note that this is cohort looks different than a pilot cohort. In the pilot you're looking to see what might go wrong, so you choose an array of users that represent your entire team, both the rough and the smooth.

In a soft launch, you're already committed. You spent the money, you took the time to implement. You're in deep, so you need to show there can be success.

But like a pilot, the key is regular checkins. Look for unexpected work, and especially ferret out if you've accidentally created any duplicative work (expecting people to do duplicative work will kill adoption).

Check that the training and the "why" of your sales pitch landed, and that it's still fresh in their minds throughout the launch. That "why" needs to stick around for as long as it takes for a new habit to form. The more compelling your "why" the less you'll have to refresh it, and by talking to these early adopters you can get an estimate of your why's half-life.

Finally: did it actually fix the problem (or look like it's on the way to being fixed)?

Easy to want to forget to check that after all the effort of implementation and rollout. But you've got to be strong and ask the question before anyone else does.

Cohort vs. Wide rollout

Ideally you can get validation from a small group of early adopters, but no matter what, at some point you have roll out to the rest of the team. Your choice here is cohort-by-cohort or all at once.

Cohorts are good if you have a limited resource like training or hardware. Cohorts let you fine-tune your rollout for each group. You also get more feedback so you can adapt and improve your onboarding each time.

Going wide gets it over with. Everyone is doing the same thing, you're only supporting one system, there's no doubt as to whether the company is truly committed to this new path.

With one big kickoff, you have a bit more of a spotlight, you can put more time and energy into your presentation and you're more likely to get some senior leadership attention, which can really help with selling that sizzle.

But iight not be up to you and you'll have to acquiesce to your People team or Enablement.

Stop adoption backslide with a dashboard & some peer pressure

Your early adopters were your handpicked cream of the crop. If anyone will adopt, it's them. But when you rollout to everyone else, no matter how good your pitch was, you'll hit pockets of resistance.

Those pockets are like a cancer. If one person or team sees a peer ignoring the change, then it's infinitely easier to ignore the change too and before you know it, your urgent and important problem isn't fixed after all.

You can prepare against this by adding adoption to the metrics you're watching (along with the metrics to show "is this actually working".)

Your instrumentation doesn't need to be fancy, but ideally it's automated and it looks professional enough to show to senior management.

A lot of companies make decks with manually created tables and one-off graphs, but my take on that is (1) it takes hours to make those decks, (2) it's hard to find those decks and (3) leaders have to proactively go open the decks. Consequently, the vast majority of those appendix slides have placeholder tables that were updated maybe one time then abandoned.

Out-of-date data is worse than useless. Not only does it not tell your leaders what you need them to know, it broadcasts to everyone that you personally are incapable of seeing a project through to its completion. Bad look.

If you take a little time and automate a dashboard, then you have a single link to point people to. Visualizations update automatically, and you now have a resource that's in the public eye ready to publicly name and shame (in a polite fashion of course) any miscreants and their managers who aren't adopting.

That dashboard needs to track "first touch" for each person turning on their software, but also an ongoing usage statistic.

If you went DIY, then check out Google Looker, a free business intelligence (BI) platform. Looker pulls data from any Google spreadsheet (as well as scores of other data sources) and it looks super-pro right out of the box. If your solution touches sales, also check out the Google Sheets add-on "SFDC Data Connector", which will pull any Salesforce report into a Google Sheet and keep it up to date automatically. Between those two tools, you can report on just about any aspect of adoption and correlate it to your problem being fixed.

This ongoing usage is a must-have non-negotiable if you're working with a vendor. Again, it has to be automated or else reporting will fall off after a couple periods.

Plan for a refresh about three months in

It's easy to let your guard down after go-live. Your early adopters were happy. Rollout went smooth. Everyone logged in. But danger lurks when you sit back in self-satisfied complacency because roll out is not a single point in time.

What's actually going to happen is you'll see a spurt of adoption at the start, then a seemingly inexorable slip back to old behavior.

Just think about your last get-fit kick. It's a curve as old as time.

When you see the first hint of sag, you need to be prepared to strike back with some fresh invigoration. Push that "why" before you start retraining, and use peer pressure (via your dashboard that all of leadership has access to) amongst front line leaders to get them to push for the behavior you want to see.

Set your sights on First Value

A successful roll out is necessary, but not sufficient. What really matters is fixing the problem, known by sellers as "first value".

This time span between roll out and value is beyond critical. It's everything for you. And here's the problem. Sellers are most naturally oriented to the Close Date, because that's when they get paid. The Implementation team is focused on Go Live date, because they're judged on open tickets. The Customer Success team only really cares about unhappy customers.

So that leaves you as the buyer all alone thinking about actual value received.

To you, the proof of concept, the diligence, the reference call, fighting for budget, negotiating all the things, legal, implementation and rollout was all a precursor to this moment: did you actually fix the problem?

To know the answer, you need to know what fixed looks like. You already worked this out in principle during the business case, but now you have to take the abstract from your business case and stick real dates on a real calendar with real metrics from real instrumentation that is really set up and really delivering real numbers.

You don't need to prove the whole problem is fixed, just that it's working. The ground beneath the pipe might not be 100% bone dry, but the pipe is mostly stopped leaking and there's only a couple more gaskets to replace.

Unless this is some massive infrastructure project, you should expect to see some proof of life within the first 90 days. So what indicators can you predict will be in place by then?

Yes it's a bunch of work to figure this all out, and at best it's anticlimactic, but the point is, this moment is on you and no one else is going to help you.

First value as a private moment of reflection

While first value should be a key milestone for you, I wouldn't make a big deal about it to the wider team. There's a very reasonable chance that your first results will fail to meet your desired expectations. That doesn't mean *you* failed, just that you learned something and you need to tweak the fix a little. No big deal.

This is a different story if you're working with a vendor. Hold those guys' feet to the fire and be very very clear that this milestone is a big deal. If they're smart they'll have an even earlier milestone so they know in advance of your milestone if they're going to land the plane or not.

   SLIGHTLY MORE EFFICIENT BUYING

I still wouldn't advertise this widely to your senior management, because if your vendor does miss the mark, it's still on you.

It's not working

If the first value milestone is fast approaching and your problem's symptoms aren't going away (or disappeared and then begin to reappear), the first response is to dig into adoption.

Is the fix not working as intended, or are people not using the fix as they were supposed to?

It's super important that you're honest with yourself on this. In reality, it's going to be a mix of the two, so by all means go ahead and iterate on the solution, but just about anything you do will need some action from your users, so stay close to your internal change champions in case they need to carry the faith for a ways while you tinker a little.

This is why instrumentation is so important. You need to be the first person to know if the fix is working or not. It needs to automated so you're not reliant on others to get your data or waiting ages only to find out the problem has been happening the whole time and you just didn't know.

Data will give you an indication where to start working on patching your fix, and it'll give you ammunition to fight a vendor who's failing to deliver and armor to defend your strategy (and your reputation) when discussing what's next internally - especially if you need more time or money before getting to the promised land.

Of course, if you nail it right out the gate, then shout loud and proud.

You rock!

Thank God I Gave You Money Day

OK.

It's implemented. It's rolled out. You hit your first value milestone more or less on time.

Only one milestone is left: Thank God I Gave you Money Day.

This is the public date circled in red on the calendar for everyone to see. The date your mutual action plan has been working back from.

It's the date that your vendor promised the problem would be fixed… and you promised the same to the leaders at your org who trusted you enough to sign off on your project.

It's the day you see the first real return, the day you know that you bet right to go with this approach. The day your urgent and important problem is no longer a problem because you fixed it.

If you went DIY, then this is the date you walk into the boss' office head held high because you delivered and you deserve some recognition.

If you went with a vendor, this is the day they should be calling you to say the same thing. Promise made and delivered.

And if they're not calling? Then either they're a bad seller who didn't actually care about you enough to confirm that their post-sale colleagues landed the plane or they're an inexperienced seller who's missing a beat. Tell them to read this book coz they're blowing a fantastic opportunity to upsell you and get a referral.

CHAPTER 6 | What's Next

Have you basked in your glory?

Made your ugly winning face at those sad detractors foolish enough to bet against you?

Magnanimously given all credit to the team, knowing that making your team look good actually makes you look even better?

You've built up some capital as a person who can spot risk, then fix it. That's a good place to be.

But before you ride off into the sunset, there are a couple of things that will make sure you get to stand on the shoulders of this success and not start from zero next time around.

It might sound big, but really it's just project management 101.

You want to be like a boy scout, and leave your company's decision making process better than you found it.

☐ Document as much as you can about your experience
☐ Do right by the people who brought you this success
☐ Figure out what's next

Credit where credit is due

Your Team

It's true. The more you praise your team, especially people below you in the pecking order, and especially people on other teams, the better you look and the more likely you'll get help next time. If there were things that didn't go so hot, take that on yourself and make sure everyone knows you acknowledged and have fixed the process so it doesn't happen again to you or anyone else. This is what leaders do and it won't go unnoticed.

Vendors

If the sales rep did good by you, kept their promises and made you look good, then take a few moments to acknowledge it.

☐ Send a note to their CRO or CEO
☐ Tell your friends
☐ Offer to serve as a reference or a case study — though consider protecting yourself with "Happy to serve as a reference a few times per quarter" so you don't get burned out.

Buying & Implementation Retrospective

This is a Friday afternoon project. The goal is to add a single page on top of your original business case documenting what went well and what could be improved.

Reread your business case and your original implementation timeline, and grab those private notes you made right after the contract was signed.

Keeping in mind that this retro will be available to leadership at your company, write down your analysis of the process and the final outcome vs. your original point of view.

- ☐ Did you get the root cause right?
- ☐ Did the fix deliver the predicted benefits?
- ☐ Did you stick (roughly) to the timeline?
- ☐ Did the fix cost more or less than predicted?
- ☐ Did implementation go as predicted? Anyone have to do surprise work?
- ☐ Do any people stand out for special thanks?
- ☐ If you had a vendor, did they stick through the entire process to Thank God I Gave you Money Day or bail before the ink was dry?

Update Your Buying Process & 11th Hour Checklist

Write down the true steps of your buying process (including your proof of value requirements and key decision makers internally) and update your 11th Hour Checklist so that you know what to ask and what to look for next time you're evaluating a vendor.

Repeat

Remember way back when you were prioritizing this problem to figure out if it was truly urgent?

Go back to that list of urgent priorities and see what's what.

Are the assumptions that drove your earlier prioritization still valid? You probably learned some stuff that might change your calculus about the true cost of change, plus there's a very good chance that what seemed oh so critical back then probably isn't as crucial now.

That's just the nature of things. Priorities change.

So what's urgent now?

What's next?

TL;DR

Hi Buyers!

You made it! I'm honored. I'll recap the whole thing in case you're actually from the Seller side and just skipped to the end to see if there's a good bit.

1. Your first priority is to figure out if this problem is truly urgent and important. That means understanding the cost this problem is imposing on you and your company.
2. Next you need to dig past the symptoms and get some clue as to the root cause.
3. Once you have some inkling of what might be going on, it's a great idea to talk to some vendors. They know stuff you don't know, and part of their business model is sharing that info to get you hooked into trusting them to buy their products and services.
4. Sometimes it pays to go with a vendor. Sometimes it makes more sense to stay in-house with a DIY solution. And sometimes the effort & expense to fix a problem is less than the cost of the problem itself. Trust in a spreadsheet to figure out both the benefits and costs of change with the different options.
5. Once you've got all the inputs, you and you alone need to make the recommendation. Whichever you go, this is on you. That can be good or bad, so make sure you're confident and proud of how you got to the decision.
6. Finalizing the decision is only step one. Implementation and rollout is where the real risk lives. Hold a vendor accountable to come prepared with expected success criteria and a mutual action plan to get there. Demand early indicators to prove that their fix is (or is not) working. Same with DIY: instrument your fix. If it's not working, make sure you're the first person to figure that out.

When all that is done, take a breath, be proud you made the world slightly more efficient, then start over.

Switch Sides

Buyers: *Go understand how sellers develop a POV about the world and think about how their expertise could make your own journey slightly more efficient*

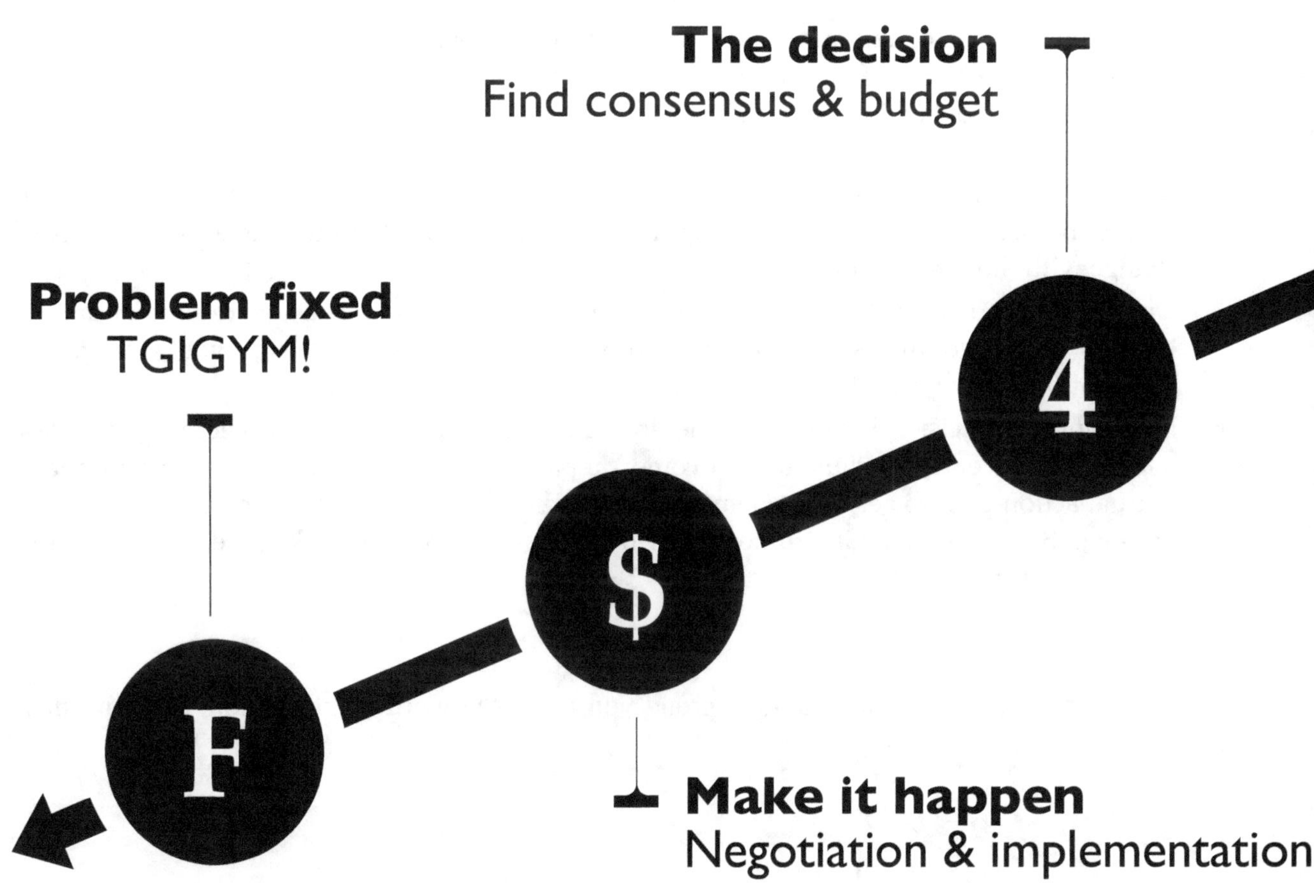